MW00619286

MY HEART IS READY

Psalm-Poems for Prayer & Proclamation

DAVID HAAS

clear *faith*
PUBLISHING

Published by Clear Faith Publishing, LLC
22 Lafayette Road
Princeton, NJ 08540
www.clearfaithpublishing.com

Copyright © 2016 David Haas. All rights reserved.

Cover art by Br. Mickey McGrath, OSFS

Back cover photo of David Haas: Kathy Baybayan

Cover and interior design by Doug Cordes

ISBN 978-1-940414-15-7

ALSO BY DAVID HAAS
AVAILABLE FROM CLEAR FAITH PUBLISHING:

(www.clearfaithpublishing.com)

Welcome, Faithful Presence:
A Week of Praying the Hours with Henri Nouwen
(Paperback edition and 3-CD audio book)

Blessed Are the Merciful:
Stations to Celebrate the Way of God's Mercy
(Paperback and Assembly editions)

Walk with Christ:
Celebrating the Way of the Nativity, the Cross, and
the Resurrection
(Paperback edition)

Praying as Living Reminders:
Morning and Evening Prayer with Henri Nouwen
(Paperback edition)

Praying and Singing as the Beloved of God
(Digital download)

For Betsey Beckman—

who,
from top to bottom,
from inside and out,
lives her life as a dancing,
living psalm of praise,
and whose heart is always
ready

CONTENTS

Foreword

The psalms are ritual windows, or maybe two-way mirrors, that see not only into the deepest joys, fears, and agonies of humanity but also into the heart of God, who is always approaching us with an invitation to better life. Often couched in personal language, these great songs, nevertheless, are the songs of a people never entirely at home in their country and never fully satisfied with their rulers or their place in the world. They have a sense that life is exile, that their king is rarely if ever the divine mediator, protector, and provider he was promised to be. The psalms know that life is hard, that real justice is rare, that friends are fickle and enemies are strong. The psalms are aware that God may be great and full of promises, but often as not seems distant, angry, or asleep. The range of human emotion, from lament to ecstasy, from "out of the depths" to "alleluia," is all there. The elation of being borne on wind, the delight of being a little tipsy, and the agony of defeat and vengeance crying for the murder of babies are all part of the emotional palette of the psalms.

What holds the psalms and the people who pray them together is one thing: memory. God remembers Israel and brings them back; Israel remembers God and follows the Torah and the prophets.

In these psalm-poems, David Haas helps us keep that same memory. In times of trouble, we remember that God saved us in the past. In our experience of God's absence, we remember that we, and others, have had that experience before, and that waiting faithfully and crying out to God will waken God to our situation. In times of joy, we remember God's justice and loving-kindness as the source of our "alleluia." Taking his inspiration from the ancient well of human longing that is the Book of Psalms, David has fashioned prayers for our moments that evoke those same acts of faith and hope that the psalms of the earlier David and other psalmists created in antiquity.

From the days of "The Lord Is My Light" and "We Are God's People," more than three decades ago, we have seen David Haas take in all kinds of insight from peers, friends, and teachers in music, scripture, sacraments, and, most recently, the spirituality of Henri Nouwen, and then with the loving art of an alchemist, create something new that is accessible and different and entirely his own. In this book, David's years of curiosity, dialogue, and prayer with the psalms have tumbled about and been pressed into these "psalm-poems." Their spiritual heart is that human desire, that "cry of the spirit," which is really nothing other than the restlessness and homelessness we feel in this exile from Eden. From within us, it is the ache to be completely reunited with the One in whose image we are made and to walk intimately again in the peaceful cool of the garden.

The wonderful thing is: God is already present in those words and images of the psalms. It was God's spirit that put them into human hearts in the first place, and who continues to radiate from within the texts and images and humanity they represent. All we need to do is speak them to join in the song that cries out on our behalf, "Abba!" Happy, sad, angry, alone; we all cry out like children for the attention of the one who says, "Call me 'Daddy.'"

And if that doesn't work, yes, "Mommy" works, too.

Rory Cooney
June 14, 2016

Introduction

It is difficult to think of any book in the Bible that speaks to the whole of the human condition better than the Book of Psalms. When we explore these pages of powerful, ancient prayer poems, it is as though we are walking down a very long hallway that's lined with a multitude of paintings and images portraying what it means to live, celebrate, agonize, endure, rejoice, lament, and give thanks and praise.

Our ancestors in faith are an incredible resource for those of us aching to live the spiritual life. Jews, Christians, and people of many diverse faith traditions find wisdom here that never seems to grow old or weary. These testimonies of the joys and terrors of life are timeless and without boundaries. Even those who profess not to practice any particular faith tradition at all find much to drink from in these wells of wisdom. For the early Christians, these prayers were so revered and honored that there never seemed a need to add their own body of specific prayers to the New Testament.

No matter what our life situations may be, the Psalter provides a true home and dwelling place for those of us who ache to be connected to God. From the opening statement of assurance in Psalm 1, all the way through to the glorious eruption of praise in Psalm 150, we travel a most precious and sacred spiritual journey.

Throughout my years as a believer, liturgical music composer, parish minister, and retreat leader, there has been no other consistent and ongoing nurturing source of energy, wisdom, discernment, and journey for the spiritual life than my relationship with the psalms. It is in that spirit—and with recognition of their importance in my life and the conviction that they are anchors for all of us in our life's journey—that I have developed these "psalm-poems." They have emerged in response to my daily life of prayer and service.

My Heart is Ready is not a scholarly translation of these ancient prayers of Israel. The psalm-poems came to life not as a result of grappling with the original Hebrew (of which I know nothing). I am a devoted student of the scholarship of psalm scholars such as Walter Brueggemann; Joseph Gelineau, SJ; N.T. Wright; Carroll Stuhlmueller, CP; Irene Nowell, OSB; Sr. Kathleen Harmon, SNDdeN; my friends Fr. Michael Joncas and Arthur Zannoni; and others. Yet while their insights greatly influenced what you will read and pray here in these pages, these what I call "psalm-poems" have primarily risen out of my own prayer and reflection, from late 2014 to the present.

These poems vary in genre and style: some of them represent a particular psalm in its entirety; others are only prayer paraphrases of selected verses; some are only taken and inspired from a single verse or a few verses; and some actually use the original psalm as a starting point and then go on to explore new rooms of prayer and reflection. In some cases, a particular psalm yielded life to two or three different poems. They are all offered here as sources for your own personal prayer life, in the context of whatever patterns you use to approach your spiritual conversations with God. The psalm-poems can also be used and adapted for public proclamation at communal prayer gatherings, according to your own local and pastoral situation.

Because the psalms have such wide arms in terms of their ability to speak to so many sacred and even nonsacred situations, I have compiled extensive indexes here that offer helpful resources for how to use this book and how these psalm-poems can serve the many different devotional, liturgical, and event-based situations that call for such prayers. At the back of this book, you will find:

- an index for the specific psalm-poems themselves;
- a prayer and special needs index;
- a liturgical, ritual, and sacramental index;
- a calendar index, to demonstrate ways in which these psalms may accompany and enrich your spiritual practices around feast days, special events and celebrations, and commemorations of people, events, and causes—both inside the traditional "trappings" of church life as well as through outreach, which can surely benefit from the deep wisdom of the psalms.

Finally, a companion resource that utilizes these psalm-poem adaptations and includes similar poetic versions of many of the biblical canticles is *Praying as Living Reminders: Morning and Evening Prayer with Henri Nouwen* (Clear Faith Publishing, 2016). The work is a four-week contemporary "breviary" of the psalms, wedded with the wisdom of Henri Nouwen.

It is my deepest hope and prayer that *My Heart is Ready* will be an ongoing and expansive resource of prayer and spiritual growth for all who explore these pages.

May God bless us on the journey! Soli Deo Gloria!

David Haas
May 26, 2016
Feast of St. Philip Neri

Psalm Poems

Happy are the ones who walk differently
than in the manner of those who heed nothing;
those who walk differently
than in the way of twisted minds—
who refuse to sit in the seat of those who scorn,
but who find absolute delight

in the loveliest of things
    and choose the beautiful pattern at all times.

For these,
these are the ones
who are like trees planted near a running stream,
that show forth fruit in their season,
whose leaves never wither away,
and whose branches stretch outwardly,
passionately.

It is not so for the wicked.

They are scattered chaff,
    blown away by the fierce wind.
They are driven, endlessly,
and will not be embraced or seen—
never gathered together with the just.

God walks with those who are just,
but oblivion awaits the corrupt.

(DH, 10/22/15, Psalm 1)

What is it that makes the nations erupt
and minds go wild?
Why does there have to be
such constant scheming?
Those with power
are filled with such arrogance
that they think
they can take on God—
and conquer the people
under God's care.

You, God,
can only laugh at their attempts.
Your anger rises up,
and you confound them.
You sit on your holy mountain
and ordain according to your choice.

Your words pronounce
and announce:

"You are my children,
 and the nations are for you alone,
 as they are your birthright.
 Today is the day of your birth,
 and you will rule with power."

And so,
 for all of you who believe
 that you can flee from God,
 listen well:

Serve God.
Joyfully, but with care.
Honorably, without greed.
Do not bring forth God's anger.

Find your home in God.
That is the better way.

(DH, 12/17/15, Psalm 2)

You are,
right at this very moment,
my children.

You are created
over and over again—
just as I am now.

All that you want and need,
I will give it.

It is yours.

But remember:
recognize and understand
what power really is.
Offer it your respect.
Rejoice in it,
but do so with care.
Revel in it,
but refrain from greed.

Happy are all of you
who find your home
in the reign of what it really is:
God's shelter.

(DH, 1/4/16, Psalm 2:7 – 8, 10 – 12, *For Dan G.*)

There are just too many—
too many
tormentors and adversaries;
they all pile up on me
and keep stabbing away.
They mock me:
"There is no hope for you."

But you—
you
are my champion,
my shield and protection.

You are the armor of brilliant light
that shines upon my face,
and you lift me up.

When I call out to you,
your comfort and safety
roll down from your holy mountain.

When I sleep,
you keep watch.

So now,
knowing this—
    I am knowing you!
    I am breathing easier,
    and my fears are whisked away
    from the surrounding panic.

You sustain me.

(DH, 11/16/15, Psalm 3:2 – 7, For Judy)

God, answer me when I call to you.
You are the one
who released me from my troubles—
so please,
continue to be good to me.
Listen to my prayer.

Look! Listen!
God confounds all who believe.
God listens when I call.

Tremble, but do not be afraid.
Be attentive to your heart,
and be peaceful throughout the night.

Pray with integrity.
Trust in God.

Those who doubt, they say,
"Who will bless us?
Even this God has abandoned us."

But you, O God,
fill my heart with more joy
than all of the grain and wine
that the cynics provide.

I will sleep secure this night.
You continue to care for me.

(DH, 9/1/15, Psalm 4:1 – 2, 4 – 9)

Listen.
Hear me.
Bend your ear,
and be the God you say you are.
Listen to my piercing heart!

I keep praying,
as constant and sure
as the daybreak,
as the sun rises each day.

At dawn
I continually place my prayer
before you.

I am waiting.

(DH, 12/16/15, Psalm 5:2 − 4)

WE HAVE HAD ENOUGH

Oh, my God.

Enough!

Stop crushing us;
ease the rage!

Have pity on us, now.
We are exhausted and spent
with this violence.
We have been cut down,
over and over.
Heal us—
we are terrified
down to our bones.

Our hearts
are more than frightened;
they are broken.

How long?
How long?
How much more?

Save us—
now, not later!
You promised,
so stay true to your word.
When we are slain,
how can we give thanks?
Why should we?

Our tears
have made us too weary.
Our grief is too much:
    too raw,
    too much edge.
The crying never seems to stop.

You violent ones—
leave us alone!

So, how about it?
Come and be the God we need,
and answer our cry.

Shame and disarm the evil.
We have had enough.

(DH, 12/2/15, Psalm 6, *For the people of Orlando*)

You are an oasis for me.
You save.
You bring rescue.

If I have done any wrong,
if I am to blame,
if I have unjustly harmed another,
then I deserve to be taunted,
overtaken,
and left to die.

And if I have done
what is right,
if I am innocent,
then soften your anger,
and bring me justice.

Bring evil to a screeching halt.
Illuminate what is good;
you know our hearts,
for you yourself are the only thing
that is true.

May you alone be praised,
because your name is
"goodness" and "righteousness."

I sing out
and reach out:

"You are God!"

(DH, 12/17/15, Psalm 7:2 – 6, 9 – 10, 18)

It is impossible
to pin you down,
to contain you,
to name you adequately.

Your name is too beautiful
and filled with glory;
it moves and dances
beyond my sight,
beyond my mind,
landing and stirring in my heart.

Your presence
extends beyond imagination
to imagination—
mystery bound,
always outward,
further and further
beyond my senses,
beyond the planets and stars.

Even the mouth of the newborn
make its wordless sounds to you—
strength too impossible to fathom,
power too mighty to ponder;
enemies brought down.

I behold the night sky
and the work of your hands:
the bright moon
and the sparkling stars
that you made.

And then I think:

Who is woman,
so frail—
that you remember her?
Who is man,
so small—
that you keep him in mind?
Who are any of us,
so insignificant—
that you care at all?

But beyond all reason,
you hold us all as angels,
as gods,
as holy!

You have crowned us
in your own splendor.
You have empowered us
    to take charge,
    to take care of your creation:

sheep and cattle,
flocks of birds,
and herds of deer,
    the goats and the cows,
and the fish
who dart about in the sea.

Your name is too beautiful
and filled with glory!

(DH, 12/17/15, Psalm 8, *For Pearl*)

My heart is exploding,
chock-full of thanks, praise, and wonder!
I proclaim you—
God of all delight!
I sing to you!

All who desire to harm me
have turned back;
see how they stumble!
You lifted me up
and kept me there—
making my cause
your cause and joy.

Your verdict for me
is very good indeed.
But you, God,
you are always alive and well,
sitting high,
yet always looking low.
Justice is your way.
All are judged by you with integrity.

The oppressed are protected.
You strengthen the weary
in the midst of every trial and trouble.

We know you.
We trust you.
You have never forsaken us.

(DH, 11/5/15, Psalm 9:2 – 5, 8 – 11)

God,
come and hear the cries
and the aches of the poor.

Listen to them.
Really listen to them.

Strengthen
their weakening and doubting hearts.
Make them strong again.

When you listen to them,
then—
the unprotected,
the fragile ones,
the orphaned and anxious—
they will know you are with them.

Justice will be real for them.

Then,
arrogance and power
will not win.

(DH, 1/11/15, Psalm 10:17 – 18)

God reclines in a temple of holiness,
and the heavens are steady in delight.
God's eyes remain focused on us—
on all of us—
with no distinctions.
God's gaze
keeps watch on the just and the wicked,
disowning and discrediting violence.
God's response?
A storm of burning fire
with burning coals hurled at evil.

Bottom line—God loves justice,
justice that restores.
Then, and only then,
will we see the face of God.

(DH, 12/16/15, Psalm 11:4 – 7, For Jim W.)

I AM CALLING OUT TO YOU

I am calling out to you.
Everything that once seemed real
    is now gutted.
No one can be trusted.
Loyalty seems to have gone far away.
Lies keep coming.
The heart appears to be absent.

God,
silence and cut off
the slippery tongues
that boast:
"Our message will win out!
What force can stop us?"

Come and boom out your response:
"I will listen
to the sighs and cries of the needy.
I will raise them up.
I will protect them
from those who want to
snuff them out and trample them!"

The words of God are pure,
   straight,
   clear,
   bright like the silver from the furnace,
   seven times over.

God,
   stay true to your promise;
   be our ongoing deliverance.
Keep us safe
   when the lies pile up,
   and when the wicked plot their course.

(DH, 12/16/15, Psalm 12)

I feel forgotten.
I really do.
Have you forgotten me?

I feel like you are in hiding—
and my grief is crippling me.
How much longer?
How much more "losing"
do I have to endure?

God,
right now,
look down and give me an answer.
Brighten the darkness
of my eyes,
and keep me from sinking.
I feel as though I am being mocked
by those who want to hurt me:
"See, you have lost again!
You are nothing!"

In the midst of all of this,
I still trust in your love
and am digging deep
to find a morsel of rejoicing
        that you really will come and save me.

While if feels as though
it is the last thing I can do right now,
I will keep singing to you,
my God,
in the suddenness of this opening,
lined with your kindness.

(DH, 12/7/15, Psalm 13)

IF ONLY

If only, if only.
If only someone
would come
and restore our freedom.

If only that would happen,
then the singing
would never stop;
the rejoicing would be endless;
and those who struggle
would find a new beginning.

(DH, 12/17/15, Psalm 14:7)

WHO WILL YOU CHOOSE?

God,
who will you choose
to welcome in close to you?
Who will you invite
to live and dwell with you
high above,
on your mountain of holiness?

Who?
The honest ones,
the just ones,
those who choose
to reveal their hearts;
those who refuse to lie—
but insist on singing
a song of truth

Who?
The ones who cherish
their sisters and brothers
and who refuse
to damage and slander them;
those who honor
their neighbor
and who honor their God.

Who?
Those who keep promises,
no matter the cost;
those who do not take advantage
of the poor ones;
those who accept no bribe
to poison or harm another.

These –
these are the ones
who will never be swallowed up,
who will never be shaken.

(DH, 12/15/15, Psalm 15)

Glorious God,
protect me.

I turn to you alone for help.

You are my God,
my all, and my greatest good.

God, you are my portion and cup,
and you give shape to my future.
You set aside for me the best of places,
to celebrate my heritage.

I offer blessing to my God
who, even at night,
teaches me; strengthens me.
God is here;
I am sure of it.
Right here, by my side.

My heart is ongoing,
always lifted, always rejoicing.
My body is quaking,
thrilled with breath—at rest.

Safe.

God, you reveal to me
the only direction that I need—
the path to life.
Joy to the most wonderful and extreme,
at your side.
Now and always.

(DH, 10/3/15, Psalm 16:1 – 2a, 5 – 8, 11, *For Gert*)

I am calling on you now.
Open your heart to my panic.
I am praying to you—
please hear me.

I long to be faithful and steadfast.
I take my steps
only upon your path.
I have not slipped.

Keep me close,
as the apple of your eye.
Disguise me
in the safety of your wings.

As for me—
I will stay faithful to you.
I will finally then,
be content in your presence—
filled with a vision of you alone.

(DH, 11/17/15, Psalm 17:1bcd, 5 – 6, 8b, 15)

THERE IS NO GOD LIKE YOU

My heart is full of love for you.
You are rock-hard strength,
my champion, my hero.

I lean on you,
for you are my only line of defense.
When I call out
I know I will be safe.
 Praise you!

You are the strong
and piercing light
that takes away the blindness
as I stumble through the dark.
With you by my side,
I can face anything.

You, simply put,
are perfect.
Your word is proven.
You offer security
to the fragile.
There is no God like you.
There is no fortress
that can hold our fear
like you do.

With you as my shield
I can see clear.
I am able to find speed
like a deer racing through the hills.
You have formed me,
and you teach me
and fortify me
for the journey.

You live!
Blessed are you,
my rock of safety!
Avenge me
when I feel broken down.
Humble all those
who come to trample me!

It is you I praise.
It is to you whom I sing.
Bless you
for your faithfulness.

(DH, 12/17/15, Psalm 18:2 – 4, 29 – 35, 50 – 51)

You have made such glory!

The heavens are the accomplishment
of your creative touch.

From the beginning of one day
to the other
your voice is clear;

from night to night,
your insight is made known.

There are no words!
There is no way to verbalize,

express, or sing adequately of such things.
They are but sounds
that move about everywhere,
to every corner of the earth;
they are profound utterances of grace
going forth to every edge.

You place a canopy for the sun—
never missing the bride.
You run from beginning to finish
as a champion would,
faster, and yet so deliberately complete.

From the starting point—
the sun is heating up, rising,
and like the runner,
it reaches its goal, its course.
For there is nothing that can be hidden
from these burning flames of glory!

God of all beginnings!
Only beginnings!

(DH, 10/27/15, Psalm 19:2 – 7, *For Rob and Mary*)

WE WILL RISE UP

Some people
brag and boast
about their weaponry
and their readiness
for battle.

It is not so with us.

We trust and we boast
in the name of God.
Nothing more.

They will fall.
We will rise up.

(DH, 12/17/15, Psalm 20:8 – 9)

God,
those who rule,
those who lead,
rejoice beyond rejoicing
because of you,
their strength.

You infuse in them
the deep desire
of their hearts.

You gift them with blessings.

Your victories—
you do not keep
for yourself.

You hand them over,
to them,
to us.

(DH, 1/13/16, Psalm 21:2 – 4a, 6)

WHY ARE YOU SO ABSENT?

God, my God,
where are you?

Why are you so absent?
Why have you chosen
to be so far away,
and leave me here—
with no answer from you,
with such a nagging restlessness
feeding and nursing my anxiety
throughout the night?

All who are near me
are mocking me,
taunting me,
and laughing at me:
 "You rely on God—
so go ahead,
let God help you now.
If God really loves you,
then let God come to your rescue."

I am poured out—
emptied,
my bones snapping like twigs,
my heart melting away,
my voice strangled,
my tongue paralyzed.
You are leaving me for dead.

Dogs and creatures
surround me,
biting at my hands and feet.
I can count the bones
of my body,
fragile and naked.
They stare,
circle round,
taking my clothing,
gambling for them.

God,
do not be so far away from me.
Be my center
and the strength of that center,
and bring deliverance
from the sharpness
of the teeth of the dogs
who hold the poison of fever
for my soul.

You do listen.
You do hear me.

And so I will sing of you
everywhere
and to everyone!

Everyone will remember
that you are present.
Everyone will honor you,
you—
absolute power
for those who know your heart.

You alone light the soul.

The future times
will sing your song
and serve you—
announcing to lives yet imagined:
    You are here!
You rescue us!

(DH, 12/17/15, Psalm 22:2 – 3, 8 – 9, 15 – 22, 23, 28 – 32)

If God is my shepherd—
and indeed that is so—
there is nothing at all that I will need.
The field of green is my resting place,
near a well of water;

my spirit is now alive again—and full.

You guide me,
true to your name.
As I make my way through
the darkest turns,
I know you are with me.

You bring a shepherd's care.

The table is laid out before me,
full and glorious,
as hate gathers close.
Oil anoints and travels
deep into the pores of my skin,
bringing healing;
cups filled, brimming.

Love will follow;
goodness will accompany me
throughout my life.
I will be brought to God's door,
and I will find my home—
my final reach.
Forever.

(DH, 11/2/15, Psalm 23, *For Gary*)

WHAT IS THIS FIRE?

Who is there among any of us
who is worthy to crawl up
to the mountain of God,
stand at its top,
and pray there—
in the holiest of places?

The one whose hands are open;
the one with a quiet heart;
the one whose soul is freed from lies,
with no deceit to be found.

These are the ones
who will be wrapped in blessing.
They are the ones
who will receive
the precious gift of God's justice.
These are the ones
who constantly seek out
God's presence,
who are pulled into God's family
and legacy.

Open up, gates of God!
Open up;

stand strong
and pave the way
for the living,
    burning fire!

What is this fire?
Who is the source
of this glorious heat?
It is God,
the all-powerful,
and ever-final,
lasting answer to chaos!

Open up, gates of God!
Open up!

What is this fire?
Who is the source
of this glorious heat?
It is God,
ever burning bright!

(DH, 12/17/15, Psalm 24:3 – 10, *For Remi*)

My soul is given freely—
and totally—
to you.

I open wide
the trust that occupies my heart.
Please,
do not close its door.

Teach me how to live.
Show me, God, your way.
Direct and point me to your truth,
you, my God who saves.
you, my God,
my endless hope.

Do not forget your tender mercy,
your endless love.

Remember the best of me,
not my flaws,
the choices of my youth.

Goodness.
Show goodness.

Remember
the very best in me.

(DH, 12/17/15, Psalm 25:1 – 7, For Cory)

My soul.
Reaching out and up.
Meet me there.

Bring clarity to my life;
guide me.
Truth-teller, teacher,
savior.
I am waiting.

My soul.
Reaching out and up.
Meet me there.

Reveal your goodness;
I am holding on for direction.

Humble me.
Bring justice.
Humble me more.
Your way then becomes clear.

My soul.
Reaching out and up.
Meet me there.

To be tethered to you
on your road
is a path of blessed kindness,
consistency,
covenant.
I honor you
and seek your holy friendship.
Your promise is my map.

My soul.
Reaching out and up.
Meet me there.

(DH, 11/29/15, Psalm 25:4 – 5, 8 – 9, 10, 14)

I keep my hands clean
as I approach
and encircle your altar—

or should I say "altars,"
the many stations
and holy places
that are the centers of your presence here.

I want to take this moment,
bask in it,
and sing like I never have before—
of all of the good that you do,
that you are.

How I love this place,
and these places
where your glory
grows, shines, expands,
endures.

(DH, 12/17/15, Psalm 26:6 – 8)

God is my living wall of light and safety.
I fear no one.
God is my sturdy protector,
guiding my life—
of whom could I ever be afraid?

When sources of darkness come together
to frighten me,
they fail;
they stumble and fall.

My heart is not afraid
of the forces that come after me
When all seems lost,
even then,
I trust.

Even then ...

There is only one thing that I ask of God—
one thing that I pray for:

to live out my life
in the house of God;
to every day

be taken up into the beauty of God,

to be pulled into prayer—
fused
and knitted tightly
within the fabric of God.

That would be more than enough.

God is relentless in keeping me safe—
from everything that desires harm,
from everything that attempts to shatter
the rock that I am placed upon.

My head is raised high
above all people and things
that are trying to choke me.

I will offer God
my entire self,
joyfully,
making music,
singing endlessly.

(DH, 10/21/15, Psalm 27:1 – 6, For Jeffrey)

IT IS IMPOSSIBLE

God, hear me.
Be merciful.
Answer.
My heart is thirsting to see you.

I do not seek anyone, or anything,
but for the gift and grace
to see your blessed face.
Do not dismiss me;
you have always been my help.

Do not leave me alone!
Even if my mother and father abandon me—
you will not.

It is impossible for you to forsake me.

Lead me, teach me your way.
Do not leave me alone with the toxic presence
of my foes.

I believe, with everything I know,
that your goodness will await me
in the places that are alive!

Wait for God!
Be strong!

Wait for God!

(DH, Psalm 27:7 – 14, For Jim K.)

Blessing!
I give my entire self—
my heart,
my ache,
my choices,
my songs,
my cries,
my trust,
my dreams—
to bless God!

For God blesses me
and sets me aside—
not as more important
but for something important.

When my help comes,
joy explodes and spills over,
and the song is so beautiful,
because God is my strength,
God is my trust.

God blesses all of us,
the people of God!
Anointing,
strengthening,
saving,
shepherding,
blessing,
carrying us into forever!

(DH, 10/13/15. Inspired by Psalm 28:6 – 9, For John F.)

GLORY!

Glory!
Give spirit-filled glory!
Glory beyond strength!
Honoring God!
Justice and holiness exploding!

Your voice
is the voice of thundering,
foaming waters!
Words that swell,
voices that boom,
all singing with glory!

Your burning voice of fire:
blasting forth with burning columns,
shaking the wilderness,
quaking the earth,
scorching the trees,
trembling with flames!

All speak of nothing but your power!

You speak above the mighty waters,
creating a new flood
of constancy and sovereignty!

You give strength to your people.
You bring peace to your people.
Blessing ...

(DH, 10/19/15, Psalm 29:1 – 4, 7 – 11, For George D.)

Come.
Reimagine
and recreate in us
a new kind of strength.

Come.

Bless us with a fresh peace.

A peace that only you can provide.

Give us this gift.

Now.

(DH, 11/15/15, Psalm 29:10 – 11)

I want everyone to know
and hear the praise
that I want to heap upon you,
for you have brought color back to my life,
after a time when there was nothing but grey.

The dim and dark will fail in their efforts.

When I was near the end of my breath,
you came with healing.
You pulled and yanked me out of the quicksand
bringing me to safety.

My soul now rests.

I also want everyone to sing to your name,
to your presence— bursting with thanks!
You will not hold on to anger,
for you spread upon me the favor of your love.

Sleep may bring tears,
but with my morning,
I will be waking with you—
joy-filled!

Take away the tears;
replace them with dancing and song.
Remove all that poisons;
and bring your balm of "happiness forever."

I cannot and will not remain silent.
My singing will continue,
my praise will be constant.
Your colors will brighten.

O God, keep me free ...

(DH, 10/27/15, Psalm 30:2 – 6, 11 – 13, *For Elizabeth*)

I will honor you.
Your name sings to me.
You reach low and pull me up.
The forces of harm
no longer have any lasting energy.

When I call—you heal.
When I search my soul— you lift.
When I sink— you rescue.

Listen, everyone:
never stop singing your psalms to God.
Give thanks, and do not tire.
God, angry?
If so (and I doubt it),
barely and only for a blinking second.
Our evening tears
are turned into a morning of endless joy.

Have mercy, God.
Help.
Take my sadness—
turn it to dance.
Remove what is dingy and stained,
and cloak me with radiance.

I refuse to be silent.
The psalms keep on coming.
Cannot contain the praise.
Impossible.
Even if I wanted to (and I don't).
I cannot imagine not thanking you.

(DH, 10/10/15, Psalm 30:2 – 6, 11 – 13, *For Ray*)

Be gracious, God,
for I feel a deep and painful ache
all over.
My eyes are tired and beaten,
my heart is exhausted,
I am filled with such dissatisfaction.

My sighs are just too deep,
so much so
that nothing else can get through.
My strength is completely tapped.
My bones are rickety.

I am insulted
over and over—
I am avoided,
forgotten,
like the dead.
I am like a horror to my friends.

But yet,
I still choose to trust you.
I still believe
without reserve or hesitation
that you hold my life
in your hands.

(DH, 12/18/15, Psalm 31:10 – 16a)

MY SECRET HIDING PLACE

You are my secret hiding place;
safety from suffering,
a freedom song,
an acclamation of rescue,
affirming my liberation.

(DH, 10/23/15, Psalm 32:7)

God's word is true;
God's words are what God does.
God loves justice and truth
and fills the earth with deep love.

God is speaking,
and the heavens are created;
God is breathing,
and the stars brightly shine.
God bottles up the sea waters
and keeps them in the deep.

Be astounded, O earth,
and stand in honor of God.
God is speaking,
and the world keeps on;
God is commanding,
and all things are seen.

God looks down from heaven
and takes notice of all people on the earth.
The creator of every human heart
knows well every human action.

God's eye remains a loving constant
on all who follow,
on all those who look to God
to bring safety in the midst of fear,
to bring rescue in the midst of death.

With all we are and have,
we wait for God,
our helper and protection.
Our hearts are steeped in joy;
we trust the name of God.

Come and love us, O God!
We are waiting.

(DH, 9/22/15, Psalm 33:4 – 9, 14 – 15, 18 – 19)

TOTALLY IN AWE

The earth moves,
totally in awe;
all mouths are dropped open
and all that lives pauses in honor.

For all that you speak

has come to be,

and all creation obeys
and submits to your voice.

All the schemes and plans of the world
are brought low,
reduced to nothing,
and the puny notions of the people
are subject to the grand design
that you desire.

Your destiny—stands forever.
Your heart's passion—
can never be brought down.

Blessed and happy
is the nation and its people
who love only you,
who choose only you,
who reach out—
only for you.

In silence,
we sit.
We are waiting for you.
Only you can help us.
You are our sturdy defense.
In you—you alone,
we find joy beyond joy.

We honor and pledge ourselves
to your unspeakable name,
for your kindness is constantly stirring,
bringing about a breeze of mercy,
a refreshing path of hope.

(DH, 11/16/15, Psalm 33:8 – 12, 20 – 22)

With all we are,
with everything we have
and hope for—
we wait,
we wait for God.

God is help and shield,
protection, safety.

Joy fills every hungry heart—
and we trust the name of God.
Come and love us, O God!

We are waiting.

(DH, 12/21/15, Psalm 33:20 – 22, *For Colleen and Mary*)

I WILL SHOW GRATITUDE

Every day, every hour,
every moment,
I will show gratitude,
blessing and thanks.

With every word I sing,
I sing of God's richness,
God's goodness—
everyone listen:
may our souls glisten
and glory together;
may the lowly ones hear,
and be filled with rejoicing!

God's eyes look out for the just,
and his ears listen to their cries.
God knows and confronts those
who choose evil,
and brings an end to their ways.

Cry out, you just ones—God is listening!
Cry out, you who are in distress—God rescues!

God is so very near indeed,
to our broken hearts.
God cries with us
when our spirits are crushed.

And God saves us.

(DH, 11/10/15, Psalm 34:2 – 3, 16 – 17, 18 – 19,
For Kathy and Glenn)

God hears the cry of those in pain.
God knows.
God's heart is lined up
and opened
to what they need.

God will take the racking pain
away from them
and will turn toward them to listen clearly
to their burdens.

God walks with them—
with the broken,
and will heal their crushed spirits,
and nurse their open and tender wounds.

God will free the innocent,
and will not allow them to be broken.
All will be safe.
God saves those who are faithful.

Rescue is near.

(DH, 11/19/15, Psalm 34:16, 18 – 23, *For Gloria*)

FAITHFULNESS WINS

When I am avenged
and gifted with a new freedom,
my friends rejoice.

Let them sing their song forever:
"God is great,
and God is pleased
when faithfulness wins out."

I will sing this song with them,
all day long:

"God is just."

(DH, 12/18/15, Psalm 35:27)

Evil conspires with evil.
Sin gossips with those
who choose darkness.
Eyes are closed to God.
Hearts are hardened
and so cannot know.
They cannot reject the dark.

Words, then,
mean nothing.
They fall out the mouth—
false and empty.
They ignore goodness,
and revel in the crooked path
and hunt out
things that sicken the soul.

But your kindness, O God,
reaches far into the darkness
of every heart.
Your integrity wins out,
stretching tall and wide
over the mountain,
and your actions stir
like the waves of the sea.

You,
you delight in life!
You are the healing stream
that renews.
You are the light
that is opening our eyes again,
as if for the very first time!

We need your protection.
We are reaching out,
with the entirety of our hearts
to rest in the soothing warmth of your wings.
We come to be fed at your table.
We come,
choking on our tongues,
hoping to taste the cool refreshment
of your living stream.

You are our fountain of life.
In you— we see the light.

(DH, 12/16/15, Psalm 36:2 – 10, *For Dad*)

Give over everything,
your entire life,
to God.
God will speak and act,
lifting you up to realize your desires.
God will touch your heart.
Delight in this.

Be quiet.
Be peaceful.
Be still and wait with patience.
God is coming.
Let go of the poison
of dwelling upon the schemes
of those who wish to inflict harm.

For those who are upright and good—
announce to them God's favor.
Peace is the only acceptable future.
God will bring this peace,
rescuing us all from trouble and anxiety.
Join God
in keeping them safe,
because they are the ones
who have trusted you.

They have given themselves totally
to the care of God.

(DH, 12/18/15, Psalm 37:4 – 7, 37 – 40)

PLEASE HURRY

I am bent over,
brought down to my knees,
and am nothing but miserable.
I feel struck by fever,
feeble and broken—
very unwell.
My groaning is deep.
My heart is weak.

God,
you know what I need.
You know all too well
the constant ache
that is trampling on my spirit.
You hear the drumming
and pulses of my heart;
my failing strength,
and can sense the blur in my tired eyes.

I feel deaf—
that I can no longer hear
or speak.
I cannot find the words
I need to say.

But in all of this,
I will wait.
I will wait for you.
I believe you care.
I trust that an answer will come.

So, come, quickly,
and bring your assent to my fears,
and be faithful.
Come now.
Come close.

Please hurry.

(DH, 1/10/16, Psalm 38:7 – 11, 14 – 16, 22 – 23)

You provide for us
a very short span of time
for our lives.

In all honesty,
we are not much at all—
we are but a mere breath;
we walk around as if but a shadow,
and our attempts
do not come to much:
we hoard after things,
but gain little in the end.

Why is it, then,
that we keep waiting for you?

We hold on to you
as our only hope
to keep us safe from ourselves
and the choices we make.
Do not haunt us
with our foolishness.

We will be silent.
We have made enough noise—
since this really is your doing,
not ours.

Please God,
end the anguish.
It feels as though
you are endlessly striking us,
and we grow weak from it all.
Remember,
we are only a breath—
fragile occupants held together
by so very little.

We are praying, God.
Are you listening?
Do not ignore us.
Listen to us!
Be attentive to our tears.
Do not keep us far from you;
we cannot bear being strangers to you.

Soften your hard look upon us,
and share a portion of your joy.

We may not last too long.

(DH, 1/10/16, Psalm 39:6 – 10, 13 – 14, *For Rory*)

O generous and wonderful You—
love all surrounding,
infinite in kindness,
lavish in tenderness—
I am confident in my security.

You have never kept your love from me,
do not hold back now.
Stop all those who seek to destroy me,
shame me,
and bring me down.
Stop them.
Do not let them win.

Let there be cheering and rejoicing,
dancing and singing:
everyone leaping and reaching
to glory You!
Your strength shines!

Even though I am humble,
poor and helpless,
you are so tender with me.
You are always my deepest help.

So come now,
do not stall,
do not delay!

(DH, 12/1/15, Psalm 40:12, 14 – 18, *For Barb*)

Blessed are we
when we cannot wait
and are anxious
to reach out to the poor.
God will then
shower us with generosity.

God will not stop
shielding and protecting us
where we live—
our enemies
will not be able to get through
to bring us down.

God will show us compassion
when we are ill—
we will be strengthened
in health
and in faith.

Let us all, together,
bless this wonderful God!

Always.
Amen.

(DH, 1/10/16, Psalm 41:2 − 4, 14)

Thirsting.
Craving.
Gasping.
Just as a deer reaches for water,
I reach—
I ache for you.
Will you come?
When will I see you?

Dry soul.
Tears—my drink.
My litany,
my crying out is endless;
where are you?

Why are you so sad?
Why the endless tears?
I can still long for you.
I can wait.
I can still praise.

(DH, 11/11/15, Psalm 42:2 – 4, 6, *For Andrea*)

God,
make your loving decisions for me,
on my behalf.
Be my defense,
and present my case
to those who are cruel,
those who want to hurt me.

For you are
my single,
my most faithful,
and my most trusted fortress.

(DH, 1/10/16, Psalm 43:1 – 2)

WAKE UP!

God—wake up!
Why are you sleeping?
God—wake up!
Why are you continually
forgetting us,
and rejecting us?

Stop hiding!
Stop turning your back;
you seem to be ignoring us—
please stop this!
Are you indifferent
to our suffering?

We are groping—
staggering to survive.
Wake up!
Help us!

We are in need of rescue.
You are supposed to love us,
so prove yourself—
     show some, right now.

(DH, 1/10/16, Psalm 44:24 – 27)

My heart is so full—
almost too full
(though that seems impossible);
It nearly bursts with the richness
of songs,
of melodies and harmonies,
of rhythms,
of music
to praise you.

Know this:
I will not hold back;
I will lift my voice
with all my skill
to announce You—
my song of love.

You are my hero;
you are the one
who takes up the sword of protection—
blaze the way
and slay all things that deny your truth.
Pierce all that seeks to deny justice to the poor.
Do not shrink from displaying your power.

Your tools for this justice are ready—
nations will shrink to your power;
the foes of justice will lose their steam.

Your rule, your justice
is as lasting as God is lasting.
Integrity.

You love justice.
You despise evil.
God has anointed you
with the oil of festival and gladness.

What you wear—is fragrant with God's beauty.
Music soars to welcome you
to the palace of God's reign—
and your heart is glad.

You are honored by the queen at your right hand.
You are arrayed in gold.

(DH, 1/10/16, Psalm 45:2 – 10, *For Joe K.*)

ENOUGH

Pay attention!
See the wonder of God!
This God of ours
is everywhere,
destroying and crushing
all hatred and weaponry of war.

Stop the fighting—now!
God is coming to break the bows;
to silence the bullets and missiles,
to burn and destroy
the vehicles and wagons of violence.

Be still!
Enough.

(DH, 1/10/16, Psalm 46:9 – 12, *For John D.*)

GOD IS OUR COMPASS

Bring your applause!
Clap your hands!
Give your affirmations
and acclamations of joy
to this incredible God of ours!

This God
conquers and levels everything
and everyone,
gifting us with our land
of dignity!

Our God,
with ease,
ascends to the top of the mountain
accompanied
by our blasts of the horn;
by our cheers of thanksgiving;
by our praise unending!

Sing praise, everyone—
to our guide and direction,
who does just that:
this God is our compass.

So,
sing out strong
to the ending point of your abilities!
Praise with everything
you have
and hope to be!

This God
sits high
but looks low,
serving the people—
God's holy people
from every corner;
with every power unleashed
toward the glory of God!

(DH, 12/16/15, Psalm 47, *For Michael and Rebecca*)

What we can see,
right here,
lines up
with all that we have been told:
This is God's city,
and God offers it protection
and lasting security.

God,
we, the people of your city,
call to mind
and remember
your tremendous,
lasting love.

Our praise,
like the holiness of your name,
lasts forever
and reaches
to every known corner of the earth.

Your right hand
holds the wonder of your justice.
Every mountain and city
rejoices with abandon!

Move throughout Zion—
move up and down,
everywhere!
Take note of every tower
and ponder deeply
the mystery of these walls—
consider and be curious about every inch
of everything!

Then,
you will be able to sing this song
to your children:
"God is here!
God is everlasting!
God cannot be stopped!
God leads us
against every kind of death—
forever!"

(DH, 12/15/15, Psalm 48:9 – 15)

All of you,
yes, you...
sit up,
pay attention,
and listen to me.

All of you,
the lowly, the rich,
all who are needy—
be attentive:

I have to share this wisdom with you,
for I can see clearly
and directly.
My ear leans toward what is true,
and I want to sing it from the rooftop!

Those only concerned with themselves—
they are lost,
and will find themselves in darkness.

But this I know—
yes, I really know:
God is my rescue.
God will guide my soul.

Even amidst the stench of death,
I will be lifted up.
I will remain fresh and free.

(DH, 12/2/15, Psalm 49:2 – 5, 14 – 15, 16)

There is not a god anywhere
who we can compare to this God,
our God—
who is constant and good
from the rising of the sun
to its setting.

God is pure light,
beautiful,
shining everywhere.

All who thank God,

honor God.
If we stay true—
we will be safe.

(DH, 1/10/16, Psalm 50:1 – 2, 23, *For MJ*)

Make clean and clear away
all of the dust and debris
from my heart.
Come and bring a steadiness,
a smooth path to my spirit.

Do not abandon me—

keep me tight to your presence.

Help me,
convince me
that joy will follow pain.

Sustain and support me;
and know
that I will provide the direction
for those who need
to return to you.

Stop the tears
so I will be able to sing a song
love-packed with the taste of you.

Provide for my voice
to clearly become a shout
of praise to you.

Courage.
Bring courage to my heart.

Sacrifices will not work.
They do not satisfy you.
So then,
I offer you my broken self:
my fragile heart,
my tender spirit.

These things you welcome.

You will not turn away,
because you have my heart.

(DH, 10/30/15, Psalm 51:12 – 19)

I WILL SHARE THIS GOODNESS

I am like a growing olive tree
in the presence of the holiest of places:
God's temple.

I trust totally in the love of God.

And so,
I will never end
my song of thanksgiving
for what God has done,
and continues to do.

God's name is good!
I will share this goodness
with all people,
at all times.

(DH, 1/10/16; Psalm 52:10 – 11, *For Jonas*)

We can be so foolish.
We can go forth about our lives
living and acting
as if there were no God.
This only leads
to choices that we regret.

God is wondering
if any of us are wise enough
to see anything beyond ourselves,
beyond our own power.

We need to lean on God alone.

(DH, 1/10/16, Psalm 53:2 – 3)

O God,
there you are –
full of judgment.
So come now,
judge me,
but judge me with favor.
Be for me—
be on my side.
Please listen,
listen to my voice:

I feel that I am attacked
by many
who can be so cruel;
many who seem
to want to bring me down,
to destroy me.

That is what it feels like.

But I believe
you love me,
     and are looking out for me.
I believe
that you want to save me.
I believe
you want to guard my life.

In the midst of the harm
that they want to bring upon me,
I want you,
I need you
to unleash your judgment
and stop them;
put an end to their cruelty!

O, how my heart
longs to be free—
free to offer myself to you
and praise your name.

You have shown me.
I see that my enemies
have turned away.
I am no longer in danger.

(DH, 12/16/15, Psalm 54:2 – 9)

Listen to me,
 I beg you; do not ignore me.
I am shaking,
and terrified.

My heart—racing.
I can feel, touch, and sense
death coming near.
I am trembling.

"If only I had the wings of a dove—
for if I did,
I would fly as far away as I could
to the wilderness
to be protected from the brimming storm."

I ask you:
stir up confusion and blur the rage,
for I see too much violence and hardship
lurking about this space
throughout the day and night.

Oppression, deception,
destruction and lies
surround,
never leaving.

But with you,
I can withstand the insults
and survive all plots
to do me harm.

Why?

Because you are my friend,
the one whom I know so well.
Always in conversation
with each other;
you keep walking by my side,
especially in dark times.

You—
my dearest
and most trusted companion.

(DH, 10/30/15, Psalm 55:2 − 15)

I WANT TO SAY

I want to say,
"Someone please give me wings like a peaceful
dove,
so I can fly away and rest somewhere
away from here— a quiet place!
I would find a patch of evening
so I could lie down,
and allow the wilderness to comfort me.

I will wait patiently,
to discover shelter from the punishing wind."

(DH, 10/7/15, Psalm 55: 8-9)

YOU KEEP YOUR PROMISES

When I am terrified,
filled with fear and afraid,
I trust you,
and in the end,
only you.

No one else.

You keep your promises.
When I remember this,
then I do not have to be afraid anymore.

(DH, 1/10/16, Psalm 56:4 – 5, *For Genevieve*)

Bring your care, O God—
take tender care with me,
as there is no place at all to hide.
Surround me with the wings of your protection.

You—you, God,
are my avenger from heaven.
Free me,
and respond in kind to those who haunt me.

Splash your love upon me
with your love that never fails,
never relents.
I am trapped with creatures
who crave to devour my body—
with cutting teeth,
with tongues like swords.

Rise up above the sky!
Spread your glory to across the earth.

They had strategies to bring me down—
nets set,
pits dug—
but they are the ones who have fallen in.

My heart is ready.
Decided.

Firm.

To you, I will sing my praise.

So everyone—
wake up the dawn!
Awaken the music for God!

My voice will come out of hiding
and sing and praise
only of you, and only for you.
Your love soars above and beyond my reach.

Rise up above the sky!
Spread your glory to across the earth.

(DH, 9/7/15; 5/20/16, Psalm 57:8, *For Katherine*)

God,
sometimes I feel as though
you are not a just God at all.

You continually allow
violence and harm
to rule the day.

The wicked seem to be too many,
and too powerful.
So many are liars,
and they attack like an angry snake.

Right now,
I want you to come and intervene—
now!
I want you to break them
and let them whither away.

I want you to not let up on them.
Keep them in darkness.
They deserve nothing better.

Because,
God,
they continue to sharpen their thorns.
So please,
come and sweep them away!

I want to celebrate victory over them.
I want you to come with your judgment!

(DH, 1/11/16, Psalm 58)

I CHOOSE TO SING

Rise!
Awake and prepare!
Come and see
this God of all people!

For me,
right now, I choose to sing,
for you are my morning strength,
my strong edifice of safety,
my haven-place,
my solace.

I choose to sing to you
for you are faithful.

I choose to sing.

(DH, 11/4/15, Psalm 59:6a, 17 – 18, *For Jo Mama*)

As I arise in the morning
I think of you.

I celebrate you!

You tower over me— strong!
You are a haven for me
when I am anxious.

Receive my song, O God,
my strong tower,
always faithful.

(DH, 1/11/16, Psalm 59:17 – 18)

YOU HAVE TURNED AWAY

God,
you promised.

You promised that you would come
and take possession of the land,
and all of us.

But you have rejected us.
Where are you?
You have turned away.

You have shaken our very foundation,
and broken us apart.
You have left us to suffer,
     and to grieve.

Come and raise your banner for us
once again.
Come and protect us—
show us now, not later.
Stretch out your hand.
Stretch out your heart
to our hearts.

Rescue us.

(DH, 1/11/16, Psalm 60:1 – 7)

Crying out, God,
crying out!

Please listen to me.
I am calling from far away,
and my courage is beginning to disappear.

Pull me closer to you
upon the mountain top,
where I can be safe.

You—refuge!
You—strength from enemies!
You—welcome!
You—home!

Keep me under your wings forever.
You have heard my pledge,
and you have held me in blessing,
the blessing of those
who have kept your name holy.

So I will keep singing, relentlessly,
each and every day.

My vow to you I will keep.

(DH, 10/12/15, Psalm 61:1 – 6, 9)

My soul is resting only in God,
and in no one else.
God alone saves and completes me;
my sturdy foundation, my safety,
my saving wall, my security.

How much longer will one be attacked?
How much more will one be beaten down,
as if they were a flimsy wall
or a weak and fragile fence?

My soul is resting only in God,
in no one else.
God is my solitary source of hope.
God alone saves and completes me—
my sturdy foundation, my safety,
my saving wall, my security.

Glory and safety— only in God.
Strength and refuge— only in God.
My friends, put your trust in this God,
always.
Let your hearts be poured out freely
at the feet of this God.

Why?

Because this God,
this God,
is the only true fountain of safety and rescue.

(DH, 10/16/15, Psalm 62:2 – 4, 6 – 9, *For Kristen*)

O God,
my ache is deep for you;
my soul and my body
are stretched to and beyond
my limit:
so dry,
so thirsty,
so desperate for you.

I am fixed on you
    so intensely,
    right there –
    in your holy place.

Radiant in strength.
Centered,
grounded in your glory.

The beauty of this life
cannot even claim a closeness
to the lavish presence
of your love.
I never can complete
what is more
than an entire lifetime of praise,
with my arms and hands
reaching out to you.
I am able to feast at this table,
so rich in its flavor,
feeding the song on my lips:
glory!

All night long,
I lie awake,
tossing and consumed
with the memory of you—
it fills my night.

You always help me,
and I am here
beneath your wings,
lost in my rejoicing;
clinging to you,
knowing that your right hand
will sustain me
while the ground churns
and turns
beneath me.

Keeping me safe.

(DH, Psalm 63:2 – 9)

We are in trouble;
we feel so unsafe.
Terror—
    everywhere.
Violence—
    consuming.

Help us.

We know and believe
that you—
if you want to,
and we know that you want to—
you can come and help us all
to make a choice for peace.
You can make the world tremble,
and discover a new way.

Then,
we will stand amazed,
in awe of your ways—
pondering,
reflecting—
and consider
what it all means.

We can reject
the notion of "enemy."

If we are just—
then rejoicing fills the air,
and a truly holy song
can and will deafen
all that is evil.

Then there will be peace.
And honest praise.

(DH, Psalm 64:2 – 3, 8 – 11)

You have won the victory,
giving completion to our prayers.
You alone,
are awesome beyond
the hope of peace
on both land and water.

With your own strength
you have steadied the fragile mountains,
and stilled the noises of the sea.
The waves that argue with each other,
the nations that rage against each other,
all troubling things
are made quiet and calm.

Everyone, everywhere
is in awe of you and your work.
From one edge of the earth
to the other,
joy fills and explodes in all things—
its shouts cannot be silenced.

(DH, 10/26/15, Psalm 65:6 – 9)

All creation,
every creature on this large planet—
needs to stand,
and shout out some joy!
Every one,
every thing—
take on "glory!"
Call on God as our
marvelous maker!

Those who defy you,
will choke and gasp before you,
while the rest of creation
keeps singing and singing!

Look at what God has done—
wonderful and awesome things for us!
The sea is turned to dry land,
and we can walk on it!

Keep the singing
        and rejoicing going strong!
Our bodies—
and our spirits—
need to dance
because God keeps all who harm us
far away.

Bless God!
Keep blessing God!
This God keeps us alive!

(DH, 1/11/16, Psalm 66:1 – 9, *For Julia*)

Care for us.
Bless us.
Shine your face upon us.
Reveal yourself to us.
Bear life in us.
Bring out praise in us.

Let all the earth know
how you keep breathing in us;
how you continually
guide all creation—
everyone, everything
follows you
to your destination,
your land of justice,
your resting place of honor.

The richness of the land
sprouts forth the harvest—
O God,
    how you have blessed us!

Do not relent—
keep the blessings coming!
And may we all
embrace and make known
our prayer of praise—
our worship to you.

(DH, 12/16/15, Psalm 67)

BLESS GOD!

Sing of God!
Make music about God!
Music, notes, rhythms—
all move to the name of God!
When we sing, God is present!
Give praise for this!

Loving parent of orphans,
and defender of the widow—
these are among the things God is and does!
The homeless have found homes,
and prisoners are led to freedom!
Those who rebel against these things,
are alone and dry.

Day after day,
time over time,
God is such a blessing!
Our burdens—God bears them all.
Saved.
Death has been conquered.

God's home—awesome, of course!
This is the God of a new Israel.
Strength.
Power.
Given to all.
Bless God!

(DH, 10/8/15, Psalm 68:5 – 7, 20 – 21, 36)

Frozen.
Stuck.
Feeling nauseous,
like I am going to throw up.

Panic.
Heart racing.
Anxious.
Cannot calm down.

I feel as if I'm going to die.

The waters are rising higher,
and I cannot calm down ...
I cannot find a foothold.

No strength,
wanting to cry out ...
long and hard.

I just want to wail.
I feel close to doing so,
    but right now,
something is holding me back.

Feeling dry.
My eyes— tired, sad.
Waiting for some relief.

God,
I'm waiting for you.

I just feel so sad.

God,
you know what is going on—
I cannot hide from you.

I just feel so awful,
so full of blame,
so responsible.

All that seems wrong
seems to be so—
      all because of me.

Panic.

(DH, 3/18/16, Psalm 69:2 – 4, 6 – 7)

Because I follow you,
because I look to you
to guide my life,
others want to mock me,
and heap their shame and insults on me.

I keep standing up for you,
and it saps my energy;
my fatigue sometimes cripples me.

I am taking the blows
for my faith in you.

Hear me.
I am praying to you.
Show me your love;
come and restore my strength.

I am waiting for an answer.
Turn to me.

(DH, 1/11/16, Psalm 69:8 – 10, 14, 17)

When we seek you out,
and surrender our trust to you totally,
we cannot help but sing:
"God is wonderful!"

(DH, 11/6/15, Psalm 70:5)

I really do believe in You.
I look to You,
now,
desperately—
do not allow me to look foolish.

I need You.
I am in need of a freedom
that only You can give—
I am in need of rescue,
for I feel danger coming near.

I need the strength
that comes only from You:
You, my fortress:
strong, firm, invincible.

Help.
Please.

Set me free
from the stranglehold
that has me by the throat.

Feeling trapped.

You are the only hope I have.
It has been so
ever since I was young.
Since my mother's womb,
You have been the one
whom I have leaned on,
over and over again.

I am now,
leaning again,
on You.

I cannot find the words
to thank You,
to praise You.

(DH, 12/7/15, Psalm 71:1 − 6)

God,
come now
    and make your position clear:
justice for the poor—
nothing less!

May the mountain of your love
bring peace to the people.

Come now,
protect your cause,
your poor ones;
save the needy—
bring a stop to the oppression!

We are holding you to your word—
that you will deliver those
who are crying out;
that you will show your compassion
to the desperate
and the helpless.

Not someday,
not some distant future possibility...
come now!
Come and save all the broken.
End the violence!

Redeem!

Rescue the ones
whom we know and believe
you love so dearly.

(DH, 11/18/15; Psalm 72:1 – 4, 12 – 14)

Justice...for all time.
Justice...empowered.
Justice...flowering.

Justice, with peace.

Peace for all people, always.
The hills shake and resonate
with the movement of justice.

May this God,
this justice, be the sole reigning force!
May this God,
this justice,
reach broadly,
from sea to sea—
to the very edges of the earth!

The needy find rescue.
The pained,
the poor,
the devastated -
are seen by this God,
really seen,
when no one else sees them.

The lowly are filled with love
and exuberance,
and desperation finds salvation.

Everyone,
bless the name of this God forever!
Keep the blessing strong
and energized
as long as the sun shines!
Everyone on the earth
will be blessed—
and every race,
every nation,
will proclaim, rejoice,
and sing of this justice!

(DH, 12/1/15, Psalm 72:1 – 2, 7 – 8, 12 – 13, 17)

I know and can trust God
when my heart is clear,
and has not grown complicated
and distracted;
when it can beat lovingly,
undeterred from the confusion
that can undo so much.

I come so close
to stumbling;
too often
I slip and almost crash to the ground.
My balance can be shaken
when the arrogance of the proud
plays the trick,
triggers me,
and hooks me in.

And so,
my heart turned hard.
My soul—cold.
My being allowed my anger
to sour my spirit;
and I felt the bite of envy.
I was so foolish.
I was blind,
so unable to see—
    so stupid.

But I returned to you.
You have taken me
by my right hand,
guided me into your house,
and shared with me
a daily awareness of you.
And here, I know the song:
The song is "Glory!"

With you, here,
delighting my life
on this earth,
what need have I of heaven?

Even if my body,
heart, and mind fail me,
I have you.

For you—
        you are my heart's center.

You are my everlasting strength.

(DH, 12/15/15, Psalm 73:1 – 3, 21 – 26)

Why?
We don't understand!
Why are we feeling so cast off?
Why does your anger rise
at us,
who are your sheep?

Why do you let the dove
be consumed by the hawk?

Stop this!
Stop neglecting us,
your very poor ones.

Rise now!
Plead for your cause!

(DH, 1/11/16, Psalm 74:1, 19, 22a)

Thanks to you,
endless thanks.

You are near.
You are present.

We touch the memory
of your doings,
your actions,
your intervening in our lives.

Thanks to you,
endless thanks.

We will keep on singing
our endless hymns to you:
songs that break the stranglehold
of the wicked,
and that empower the just.

Thanks to you,
endless thanks.

(DH, 1/11/16, Psalm 75:2, 10 – 11)

Listen,
all of you
who say you honor God:

Keep your promises.

Bring and share lavishly
the gifts that God has given you—
and give them back to God.

(DH, 1/11/16, Psalm 76:12)

My eyes,
my heart—
feel nothing but torment.
My soul is refusing
any comfort or peace.

I think of you,
and I cannot stop moaning.
During the day I keep aching for you.
During the night I keep reaching out
and feel as though you are not grabbing on.

My spirit is crushed
when I think of my life.
You seem to render me mute
when I long to speak.

I remember the past,
the times and days gone by—
mistakes, wrong choices,
repressed joy,
acts of shame.

It all haunts me.

Are you prepared
to leave me here alone,
rejected forever?
Have you stopped loving me?

Have you forgotten
to be merciful?

Is your anger that hot?

No hope for restoration?
No healing?

(DH, Psalm 77:1 – 10)

Do not keep the story hidden.
Do not let it remain mute.
Our children must hear and know about this God
and learn of all the incredible things God does!

Pass on to the next generation
the endless blessings.
Teach the young
to live their lives in trust—
that they are not alone,
that the Holy One is always walking with them.

Covenant fulfilled...
Promises kept...
Hope sustained.

Never, never forget.

(DH, 11/27/15, Psalm 78:4 – 7, For Art Z.)

WE ARE YOURS

We belong to you.
We are yours.
We are your living thanksgiving.

We are your unending,
relentless,
untiring,
and always passionate,
song of praise.

We are yours.

(DH, 1/11/16, Psalm 79:13, *For Anthony*)

Turn our hearts around.
Shine.
Enlighten.
Open us up.

Listen and be our shepherd.
You live in the distance
with the angels—
come close!
Shine and don't hold back;
        keep the light beaming!

Come back to us,
come down from your heights
and think of us,
we, your vine,
and water us,
protect us,
for you are the one who planted us.

Our roots are dug deep in you.

Reach down with your right hand
upon us,
your chosen,
who are strong,
all because of you.

We will not turn from you.
Breathe your life
back into our breath,
and we will call out to the world,

singing and celebrating you,

and you alone.

Come, now.
Revive.

(DH, 12/15/15, Psalm 80:2 – 3, 25 – 26, 18 – 29)

I keep singing.
I keep singing to you,
God,
my unending strength.

I chant my psalm to you,
and I do so
with all my heart.

I strike the drum,
strum the strings,
and I blow the horn
at the New Moon!

For this is the appointed day,
a time for feasting!

(DH, 1/11/16, Psalm 81:2 – 4, *For Jackie B*)

TAKE UP THEIR CAUSE

All other idols,
all false gods,
will stand in judgment
before God.

God confronts them.

End your support of evil!
Stop siding with the wicked!

Rather,
choose God's rule:

Bring justice to those orphaned,
those suffering from injustice;
uphold their rights
and take up their cause!

Walk at the side of victims—
the voiceless who cry for freedom!

But be strong
in rejecting the presence of the demons
who wander in the dark,
allowing the world to keep breaking down.

Let God arise!
Let all people,
everywhere,
have their empty places filled!

(DH, 1/11/16, Psalm 82:1 – 5, 7)

Rise up, God!
All nations, all people,
belong to you!
Uphold and speak up
for those who have no voice!
Bring freedom, bring justice!
Be sure rescue for the poor,
and free them from harmful hands.
Lift up the weak;
heal their aching spirits.
Rise up, God!

(DH, 11/11/15, Psalm 82:3 – 4, 7)

O God,
do not hold on to your silence,
do not hold on to your stillness.
Open your ears to hear us,
do not deprive us of your voice.

Listen to the stirrings of those forces
that rise up against you.

O God,
reduce any opposition we have
to the power of straw
held against the whirlwind.
Stoke the fire
and let it burn all things down
that move against you.

Bring about a storm that truly humbles—
that will bring our egos to the ground.

Let us all know,
once and for all
that you alone are God;
that you alone hold the name
that is above all
in all
and through all.

O God,
do not hold on to your silence.

Do not leave us alone.

(DH, 10/19/15, Psalm 83:2 – 3, 14 – 19)

I ACHE TO BE THERE

Your home.
Where you live.
Beautiful.
I ache to be there.

My whole heart,
my entire body,

sings –
sings to you,

my living God.

Even the smallest of birds
find a place for a home,
a space
to land, to settle.

They can open up
and serve their young
at your table of life;
your heavenly regiment
serves—
my God.

My dear God.

To live and linger with you
is such a blessing;
a most precious joy
that goes on forever and ever.

To hold the courage
that you provide
settles our hearts
to make the journey.

One moment with you—
a single instant—
is so much more
than thousands deprived.

I long to settle at your door
rather than to move among those
who bring fear and wrong and hurt.

Sun.
Guide and guard.
Grace and honor—given.
Never holding back,
generously blessing
those who live in the right.

You and your holy sentinels
are most sacred indeed—
and given due loyalty
from all who place in you their trust.

Security.
You.

(DH, 11/3/15, Psalm 84:2 – 6, 9 – 13)

Hear me,
and listen to my prayer.
Be present and listen.
Look upon me,
pay attention and see

the face of your anointed.

Be here.

One day,
just one day with you
is better than a thousand or more
without you.

I would always hold out
rather than dwell with those
who would bring harm.

God is our sun,
our shield,
our source of honor and grace.

God will never hold back blessings
to those who walk with justice
and integrity.

(DH, 10/24/15, Psalm 84:9 – 12)

OPEN UP LOVE

God,
you look kindly
upon our parched land;
upon our dusty hearts.

Forgiving shame,
cleansing us of all fault,
controlling rage,
shunning anger.

Come to us,
but not in anger or fury!
Come to us,
with grace and tenderness.

Pierce our dryness
and bring forth lives that blossom.
Breathe life into your people,
your "no longer abandoned,"
and cover us with your joy!

Forgive.
Restore.

Come and revive.
Draw near and nourish.
Come close.
Show mercy.

Open up love.

(DH, 10/26/15, Psalm 85:2 – 8)

I will take a moment.
Stop.
I will listen to what God is saying to me,
right here, right now.

God is speaking that we might listen:

Peace.

Peace to all people—
to those who keep faith
and for all who lean their hearts
toward God.

We can be saved from our terror,
if we would only honor God
and what God honors—
then glory can
and will
dwell among us.

True mercy, love,
and faithfulness are real.
Justice and peace have embraced,
and their relationship is sealed.
Fused together—cauterized.
Unbreakable.
Faith is bursting forth from the earth,
and all that is just is hovering over us,
providing a canopy of protection.

God will keep blessing us,
and all living things on this earth
will welcome in this blessing,
with justice leading the way,
guiding the way of God
to interrupt our ways.

(DH, 11/16/15, Psalm 85:9 – 14)

I am clinging on to a final hope.
That hope is you.
I am nearly completely broken.

My faith is fragile;
my trust is weak; my life is vulnerable;

but my faith in you remains.

Give me courage, God.
I need you so much,
and I am crying out constantly.
Refresh my soul,
as I give my life over to you.

You are good.
You are pardon, healing, and grace.
Please come quickly,
take on my life
and drown me with your mercy.
Hear my voice—listen to me.

I know as much as I know anything
that you will catch me in my falling.
You will heal me in my fearful state,
because you are my amazing miracle:
the hope
that I have been searching for to believe in.

Nothing,
no one—can even barely come as close as you,
in entering into the mix of my dreams;
lifting me up to believe in them.

Because it is you
who opens and strengthens my weary eyes
to really see with a fresh clarity—
as though for the very first time—
    that such dreams are not to be laughed at,
    but rather,
     embraced as storylines
    that can and do come true.

(DH, 1/13/16, Psalm 86:1 – 8, *For Kathleen S.*)

We all have our "Zions"—
our holy mountains
that are created by God,
that greatly surpass
all other places
in the Israel
of our own homes.

Glorious things happen
and are spoken at these places.

These are places of wholeness.

Birth.

Born from these "Zions."
And God sustains this wholeness;
he guides and protects.

God knows our names,
and keeps a record of our birth
and rebirth.

Such wonder we have seen,
and so we sing and dance
our way home.

(DH, 1/11/16, Psalm 87)

I now know
that you are my life,
and my only help.

From the distance at day,
I cry out to you.
At night—
I am here,
vulnerable,
waiting for you to come to me.

May my prayer touch you—
and open your ears
to hear me.

I keep reaching out to you
all day long—
    my hands are outstretched,
    wondering where you are.

Do you not work wonders?
Do you not bring light to the shadows?

My eyes are burning,
my heart is straining to find you.
Every morning
    I wake up,
and keep offering
this unending prayer to you.

Why are you throwing me aside?
Why are you hiding?

Your anger is like a fire
sizzling throughout my body.
I am devastated
by the trials you put me through.

My anxiety is swirling everywhere.
I am drowning.
Pulled down to the bottom.
Feeling closed in.

Can't breathe.

You have stolen my companions from me.
The light has been taken away.

(DH, 1/11/16, Psalm 88:2 – 3, 10b – 11, 14 – 15, 17 – 19)

From the earliest hours of the morning
until the last dimming of night,
I will sing relentlessly of your kindness.
Passing through every generation
I will make it known

that your faithfulness is infinite,
without end;

patterned to outlast heaven itself.

The vast sky is the praise of your wonders,
the stars above and beyond—your tireless love.
How and where can the heavens measure you?
Who out there can even come close to being like
you?

How blessed and happy are those
who are pulled in, so near to your light!
The music of your name—a most joyous song,
and your justice, a most precious gift.

I am safe in the embrace of your promise,
a covenant that will last throughout all time.

(DH, 10/4/15, Psalm 89:2 – 3, 6 – 7, 16 – 17, 29, *For Katie*)

Come back.

You keep things steady.

We hold on to you
from forever to forever.

Before there were mountains,
there was you.
Before any beginning,
middle or end, there was you.
You have always been
our God, forever—
    before any beginnings were imagined.

You.

Come back.

Time is lost on you.
Your eyes are like a thousand years
that have come and gone over and over
without any beginning or ending.
Time has come and gone—
night and day like yesterday,
and again—gone.

Come back.

Why must we wait?
How long are we to endure?
Why are our days numbered?
Come back.
Soon.

Fill us at dawn,
fill us as fully as you can
with a love and energy
that can transform our pain
and bless us with joy,
making us whole again.

Come back.

All need to know—
all of us who serve you,
the old and the young.
Let your love shine all over us—
on our work, bring success;
all of our work for ourselves,
each other—and You.

Come back.

(DH, 11/6/15, Psalm 90:1 – 2, 4, 13 – 17, *For Marty*)

All of us who know God's shelter
and rest in God's shadow,
sing to God in hope:

"You are my trust."

God will pull away
all people and things
that hunt you down,
that hold you imprisoned.
You will be covered
with wings that will keep you safe.

You will not be haunted by the night.
You will not be the target of arrows.
You will find your steps at nighttime.
You will not suffer harm at noon.

In the midst of the killing of thousands,
you shall live free,
unscathed;
kept innocent by God's protection.

God will shut out
everything that may cripple your life.
No more harm will come to you.
Angels are keeping watch.

Your feet shall pass over stumbling stones,
for these are strong angels
who are always protecting you.

God announces:

"Whoever holds on to me,
I will set free.
Whoever knows me
and calls me by name,
I will answer them,
and stand by them,
no matter what,
in the best
and in the most frightening of times.

I will always be their rescue.
I will give them life to the full—
I will have their backs;
I will be their safety."

(DH, 1/11/16, Psalm 91:1 – 7, 10 – 16, *For JMJ*)

It is so good—
     even though it is challenging—
     to give thanks and praise
     to your unsayable name:

In the morning light
we remember
your amazing kindness;
with the night sky
we call to mind and ponder
your most faithful heart.

We sing about these things
and so much more
with every instrument
we can get our hands on,
because every deed of yours
demands a song!

Every thing you do
     is stunning;
     you are at work in everything,
     and we become animated
     by your stirrings—
     too deep to comprehend!

To not be taken in by you
is to be utterly foolish.
There are scoundrels out there,
springing up like weeds.
They begin to bloom,
but they cannot sustain any growth—
thus they are mowed down.

But you cannot be mowed down
because those who oppose you
    become scattered and are cast away.

You strengthen us,
    and anoint us with new resolve:
    we glisten and grow,
    brighten and glow,
    and are given fresh eyes
    so we can see clearly;
    fresh ears
    so we can hear
    and tune out
    the noise of those who bring harm.

So we will grow justly,
like palm trees!
We will rise up majestically
like the cedars of Lebanon!
We will be planted in your house,
our leaves eternally green,
rustling in your courtyard.

Even though we will grow old,
our branches will flourish,
stay vigorous,
covered with foliage.

We will remain your emblem of justice.
We will be sealed
with no possible cracks to be found.

(DH, 1/11/16, Psalm 92)

God is in charge.
God reigns.

God's robes cover
the earth with goodness
and strength.

The vast cloth of God
is a gift
wrapping with power—
and the world watches firmly,
    not afraid,
    not shaken,
    but welcoming and opened
    for God's direction,
    a most ageless path.

Onward roll the tides
    and the surging waves—
    like the crack of thunder,
    relentless,
    intense,
    unrelenting.

Energy!

Sailing and crackling
above the waters,
higher than the breakers—
God rising,
God who is mighty,
God who rules.

God's commands are eternal

and cannot be brought down.
Holiness is everywhere,
holiness enlightening!

(DH, 12/9/15, Psalm 93)

God,
be our light,
our avenging presence!
Shine on,
rise up,
make things clear.

Shatter the darkness
with your judgment,
open up and reveal
all of our arrogance,
all of our strutting,
all of our boasting,
all of our flaunting.

Do not allow us
to crush your people;
bring to a screeching halt
our actions
that tarnish your heritage.

Correct us,
and teach us
to see with your eyes
and to hold your thoughts.
You certainly know
our thoughts,
and how they clash with yours.

And yet,
you simply refuse to desert us.
You will not and cannot tolerate
our being abandoned.
It is impossible for you
to forsake us,
because we,

we are your heritage,
your legacy,
your living sign
that you exist,
that you are real.

Justice will return to justice.
Peace will prevail
when honesty is nurtured.

Who will speak up for me
when I continually falter,
when my weakness
and predictable flaws
keep springing up?

You will.

Without you as my center
I would become and remain numb.
When I feel as though
there is no ground beneath me,
your love keeps me steady.
When my anxiety boils,
you bring a healing quiet.

You are my every comfort,
my rock of protection,
my hope of justice—
my new and renewed character.

With you I am whole.
With you I am home.

(DH, 1/11/16, Psalm 94:1 – 6, 10 – 11, 14 – 19, 22 – 23a)

So here we are:
singing to you—
infused with passion,

leading and erupting

becoming a shout:

Here!
Now!
At the place and space
where you are present!

We are totally taken
with and by you,
possessed by you,
belonging to you.

So here we are:
We celebrate You—
because you are the gift of power,
a power that no one
and no thing
can match.

You have the hands
that touch the depths of the earth.
You are the heart
that pierces the mountain's height.

You are the presence
that constantly changes the sea
because it is yours—
it belongs to you.

So here we are:
in awe,
bringing the earth and the sea
of very selves
to you, here,
now.

You are the beyond that we follow.
We are the doing—
the sheep who graze,
close to you,
inviting you to come
and shape us,
and change us.

So here we are:
listening to your voice,
hoping to be awakened
and shaken by your word—

"Do not lose heart
as you have before,
when you became confused
with the afflictions
that surrounded you;
in the days when your parents
all but lost their faith
as they demanded outward signs
of everything that already is:
my presence.

For forty years
I became and remained bitter,
because they became
a lost people,
blind to my destiny for them.
I then made a vow,
in anger,
that they would never again
enter my house."

So here we are:
in light of all of this.

Here we are.

(DH, 1/5/16, Psalm 95, *For Paul*)

Join me
and join this most blessed earth
in singing a new song to God:
a new melody
with fresh and daring harmonies
growing and blooming
and bursting,
singing and praising God's name!

Bring with you
a daily portion of phrases
and rhythms
that save!
Sing this song everywhere,
sharing God's miracles,
proclaiming God's wonders!

God is awesome and great—
sing about that!
God is honored
by our tremendous displays
of power—
for it is God alone who designed the heavens,
who had sight put on the stars,
and who marked the night with light!

Everyone, listen!
Recognize this light!
Bathe your faces in its blinding brilliance!
Place yourself in the center of it all
 and recognize what a gift it is!

Then the trees throughout all creation
will brim strong with dignity –
greening more and more
with praise to this God
who is coming,
coming to bloom with justice;
coming to take hold of this world,
and infuse our hearts
with the sweet gift of truth.

(DH, 12/15/15, adapt. from Psalm 96:1 – 6, 11 – 13,
For George M.)

GIVE THANKS

God reigns!
Everyone and everything on earth
can taste it!

God is here!
The clouds gather to rain down,
to drench the earth with integrity!

God is blazing!
Flickering and moving,
burning up all that tries to resist!

God sees!
The mountains and hills melt
and begin to slip away—
the flames clarify everything,
clearing the brush;
creating a path!

God is loud!
Justice and righteousness
exploding wide open,
reaching everywhere!

God blooms!
Light sprinkles about,
bringing joy to every heart
eager for what is right.

We can see it!
Give thanks!

(DH, 11/12/15, Psalm 97:1 – 6, 11 – 12)

Good looms,
>   blooms,
>   and booms over the earth!

The earth—gladness and rejoicing!
The many islands—gladness and rejoicing!

God comes
surrounded by the cloud and darkness;
justice creates the foundation
of the reign of God.

God heats up
and blazes—
with lightning and thunder
trembling the world,

all that is evil.

Mountains melt,
dripping like wax
before God's face.
The glorious skies
sing and brighten
the justice of God.

We,
loved by you,
reject and renounce
darkness and sin.
You embrace us
and guard our souls,
opening the doors of freedom.

Light—everywhere!
Joy—everyone!

All of us,
all creation,
give you thanks
for the holiness of memory.

(DH, 12/9/15, Psalm 97:1 – 6, 10 – 12)

God:
Victory is made known.
Justice is revealed.
Mercy,
blessed mercy—
is never forgotten;
it is ever loyal.

Always faithful.

(DH, 12/8/15, Psalm 98:2 – 3)

Even though
we are sometimes lured
into thinking we are—
the truth is
that we are not God!

We are not in charge:
God is.

God reigns.
When God speaks,
all creation responds:
with trembling and shaking.

It is not so much that we are good
that drives us to celebrate.

Rather,
it is because of the blessed fact
that God is good.

(DH, 1/11/16, Psalm 99:1 – 3, *For Stefano*)

Break through!
Shout out, all the earth!

Serve!

With glad hearts—
approach God and sing!

It is God—yes!
It is God who made us.
We belong to God;
we are the flock who follows!

Come enter through the door
with everlasting thanksgiving.

Come in, everyone,
with singing to the name of God:
Holy! Give thanks!

God's goodness never ends,
and is faithful always.
From the beginning of life
through the life after life,
no one can put a stop
to God's goodness,
God's mercy,
God's amazing love!

(DH, 10/25/15, Psalm 100)

STEP BY STEP

My song,
my music,
is the tonality of justice and love.

All that is alive and all that is true
drives my rhythm,
and it transforms
the central nervous system of my life
into an energy
that is consumed with you.

So, where are you?
When you will come to me?

I will move step by step
with a blameless heart;
I will shun what is false—
not allowing it to come near.

I want the loyal to dwell with me—
those who live in deceit
are not welcome.

Every morning,
today,
and tomorrow's tomorrow—
I ache to purify
and restore God's glorious city.

(DH, 11/28/15; Psalm 101:1 – 3a, 7 – 8, *For Raymond K.*)

From ages past
you made, built,
and crafted this earth.
The sky and the heavens—
they too—
are among
your many tremendous compositions.

But even if they fade,
you never will.
You only become more present.

While our clothing
becomes old and tattered
and eventually thrown away,
you will never wear out;
never grow thin.

You remain.
There is no "final time" for you.

(DH, 1/11/16, Psalm 102:26 – 28)

BLESS GOD, MY SOUL

Bless God, my soul,
and all that is within me,
give blessing!

Bless God, my soul,
and never forget the blessings—
this God,
who forgives us from all our demons,
who heals us in our disease,
who redeems our life, always lifting up,
who crowns us with infinite love and mercy,
who satisfies us with all that is good,
always,
so that our youth is restored
like that of the eagle.

God brings righteousness
and justice for the oppressed.
God's ways are made known to Moses,
and God's actions are centered in Israel.

God is merciful,
gracious,
always slow to anger,
abounding in steadfast love.
God will not always accuse,
nor is anger held close.
God does not haunt us with our sin,
nor respond back to us in kind.

As high as the heavens soar above the earth,
so great is God's love shown
toward those who stand in God's honor.
Just as far as the east is from the west—
so is the mercy that God grants and casts away
from our hearts.

As fathers and mothers have compassion
for their children,
so does God have compassion for us,
for us who honor God.

God knows how we were created.
God remembers that we are dust.
As for us, our days are like grass;
we flourish like a flower of the field.
The wind passes over it,
and it is gone;
it no longer knows its place.
But the everlasting and infinite love of God
is from everlasting to everlasting
on those who honor God,
and righteousness is given lavishly
to children's children,
to those who keep God's covenant
and remember God's holy law.

God has established reign in heaven,
and guides and leads everyone.
Bless God, all angels
and all who are mighty and powerful,
always obedient to God's word.

Bless God, all who surround,
all ministers who follow God's way.
Bless God, all wonderful works,
in every time and place.

Bless God, my soul!

(DH, 8/31/15, adapt. Psalm 103, *For Bonnie*)

My soul is a welcome place for your blessing.

All that is within me
yearns and aches to bless your evasive name;
far too holy to contain;
far too deep to remember;
all of your gifts brimming over—
it is too much to hold.

My soul is a welcome place for your blessing.

You God,
you God, who forgives everything,
who heals everything,
who redeems everything,
who crowns everything
with a tireless love;
who satisfies;
who is kind
and full of mercy,
who awakens and refreshes all time
and continually buds forth
the feather of an eagle—forever young.
You are forever full of promise.

My soul is a welcome place for your blessing.

You God,
you God, who is just when everything
and everyone else seems unjust.
You God,
who holds Israel close,
through Moses our gentle and firm teacher.

You: kindness.

Graciousness.
Mercy.
Anger falls away.
Love enters, new and bright.
You dwell with us, not accusing;
refusing to haunt us with our sin.
Never returning our brokenness with more
brokenness.

My soul is a welcome place for your blessing.

As high as the heaven can possibly be
above this earth,
so far and wide is your kindness.
You God,
you God, who transforms our weakness
from one far end to the other,
are always healing, always loving.
Our failings are sent so very far away.

My soul is a welcome place for your blessing.

As a parent, ever so compassionate,
you God,
you God, redefine and recreate compassion,
for those who show honor.
You God,
you God,
you know who we are;
never forgetting we are like the dust,
and the dry grass,
pushing out the flower in the field,
for only wind passes through,
and it is gone.
The field quickly forgets.

My soul is a welcome place for your blessing.

But you God,
your love stretches and looms
from forever to forever.
From you, righteousness flows from us
to our children,
and our children's children—
for those who keep faith with you;
for those who keep moving with you.

You, God.
You God, sit high while looking low,
deep into the center of all things,
embracing everything,
blessing everything and everyone.

My soul is a welcome place for your blessing.

Let us bless this God—
heavenly creatures, messengers all;
all who are hospitality and home,
all servants who build up this God's command.
Let us bless this God—
from all that has been made,
for all that is,
throughout all time,
throughout all places.

My soul is a welcome place for your blessing.

(DH, 7/19/15, Psalm 103, *In memory of Carrie*)

Mercy!
Bless God, O my soul!
and all that is possible within me,
bless God's most holy and blessed name.

Mercy!
Remember always, the blessings of God—
the one who forgives your shortcomings,
the one who heals your afflictions,
the one who redeems your life from the pit,
the one who crowns you with unending love and
compassion,
the one who satisfies you with only good things,
the one who does so forever,
the one who soars within you like an eagle,
the one who restores your youth.

Mercy!
This God is a God who brings forth justice
for those who are oppressed.

Merciful.
Gracious,
Slow to anger.
Abounding, bursting forth with love.

Mercy!
This God will not pile on shame and guilt.
Anger lasts barely a moment.
This God does not deal with us according to our
failures.
This God has not, does not, and will not
haunt us with our sins.

Mercy!
As high as the heavens are,
that is the height of God's love
for all who return to God their honor.
From the rising sun in the east,
to the setting sun in the west—
this is the length and breadth of the restoration
that God provides.

Mercy!
As loving parents have compassion for their
children,
so does this God, have compassion for us.
God knows us, better then we know ourselves.
God remembers how human we all are.
For the human soul—our days are like the grass—
flourishing like the beauty of the fields.
The wind passes over it, and suddenly it is gone.

Mercy!
God's love—now, God's love
is from everlasting to everlasting
for the faithful ones,
those who keep God's covenant,
and who cherish God's commands.

Mercy!
God sits high,
but looks and loves—low.

Angels—bless God!
Those with power—bless God!
All who minister to the light—bless God!
All wonders and works—bless God!
Everyone in all places—bless God!

Bless God, O my soul.

Mercy!

(DH, 7/28/15, Psalm 103)

Amazing!
You have created so much—
you have created it all!
The earth is bursting
with all of your creatures—

with all of the ferment and movement

that is stirring and buzzing about.

The sea is wide and vast
and the creatures it holds
are too many to number—
all things that live and breathe,
small and great.

Everything looks,
and points to you
        to nurture them
        when the time is right.
You offer it,
        and they all pull it together
        and gather it up.
Your hands are wide open—
filling everything.

When you hide your presence,
they are sad.
If you take away their very breath,
they die—
    and return to their dusty beginnings.
But when your spirit blows and turns
and enters their spirits—
all is made new!

The earth is renewed!

(DH, 11/18/15, Psalm 104:24 – 30)

ALL OF THESE

Praising!
Thanking!
Remembering!
Blessing!
Alleluias!

All of these
we shout out to you!

All of these
we attach to your name!

All of these
we raise up to you in song!

All of these
we lavish upon you!

All of these
radiate our delight in you!

All of these
recognize your power!

All of these
celebrate your presence!

All of these
remind us of your signs and wonders!

All of these
come from us, your chosen people!

(DH, 1/11/16, Psalm 105:1 – 6)

Thanks!
Give God thanks!
God is good
with mercy unending.
Who can tell the story of the acts of God,
or total up the praise due?

Blessed are all when justice is chosen,
who make the choice for right, always.
Remember me, O God,
and show your favor to me,
as you do with all your people!

Accompany me with your power that saves,
that I may see and take in
the blessings of your chosen people,
the bounty of rejoicing,
boasting always in your glory!

Be here, God,
right here and right now!
Gather us together from every place
so to give our gratitude loudly—
your name, filled with glory!

May it be so for us all to praise you!

(DH, 10/16/15, Psalm 106:1 – 5, 47)

Let us spill over,
brimming with thanks—
for your
"impossible to understand"
love and care for us.

For you—
you shatter and blast apart
the irons and shackles,
all the doors of copper:
you have hacked them all open.

Our cries do not fall on deaf ears.
You hear us.
You listen.
And you answer
with a bolt of healing,
with thunder
and an unending pulse—
keeping us alive!

You bring a hush
to the wind;
you tame
the waves of the sea;
the winds that knock us down
and the waters
that drown the joy—
they are no match for you.

You quiet the restlessness,
and turn the desert into spring.
The hungry are filled;
the city is restored.

All of us
who are of good heart—rejoice!

Take it all in—
digest this wisdom:
the wisdom of God's love.

(DH, 1/6/15, Psalm 107:15 – 16, 19 – 20, 29 – 31, 33 – 36,
42 – 43,
For Zack and Natalie)

I have decided,
for my heart is ready;
ready to sing and offer praise.
My harp and lyre are prepared
and so I can—
and I will—
wake up the dawn.

My voice is lifted and freed
to sing about you, God,
to everyone, everywhere -
about your endless love,
mercy,
and truth.

Even the skies will hear my song!

Rise high above the tip of heaven!
Fill the earth with your boundless glory!
Bring deliverance to all those
whom you love.
Come now, and deliver us all!

(DH, 10/15/15, Psalm 108:2 – 7)

God, be true and kind to me.
I am in need of rescue.
I am wounded,
O so very wounded;
and my heart is bent,

pierced and broken.

Help me,
rescue me, God.
Let everyone see
that you make this happen,
that you alone have done this.

My voice,
my song is raised to you.
Thanks is given,
and I will continue to give it.

I make music for the crowd to hear—
for you, God,
stand by your people
and me,
your wounded one.

I, all of us,
    are safe with you.

(DH, 10/29/15, Psalm 109:21 – 22, 26 – 27, 30 – 31,
For Becky G.)

For all of us who dare to lead,
we need to remember
that any power that we have
is grounded in God's covenant.

Only then,
will we have the loyalty of the people.

If we remember this,
then the people will be one with us,
and stand with us.
Then our power is truly holy,
renewed and fresh,
and born again like the dawn.

God gives us this most blessed oath:

"You are my servant, forever;
because I have made it so."

(DH, 1/11/16, Psalm 110:1, 3 – 4)

Not halfway,
not mere lip service—
but with the entirety
and fullness of my heart,
I want to,

I must,

praise the God of justice.

Digging deep,
I know that God's actions
are a delight for my heart:
for God's justice is real,
sturdy,
dependable.

Who could ever forget?
This God,
kind and merciful,
nourishing always,
keeping promises,
manifesting glory
and making the land fruitful.

God's commands
are full of truth.
God's commands
are brimming with justice.
God's commands
are to be trusted.

Forever.

We are holy by God's hand,
and faithfulness
is the result of God's actions!
God's name must be honored.
God's name must be given praise.
If we truly seek wisdom,
we will see God.

Give Praise!

(DH, 12/2/15, Psalm 111)

Every corner,
every crevice of my heart
praises God among the just.
God's works are great
and bring delight.

Great beauty and brilliance—
they frame the portrait of God's justice.
A true testimony is sung
of mercy and grace, everlasting!
Who could ever not remember?

This God
has kept promises,
revealed great things;
God's word never fails to provide.

Trust.

God's faithful ones will last
beyond all lasting things;
they are created from a love
that is strong and true.

God's name: Holy!

And so we are as well—
       wise by God's direction,
       blessed by our choices.

Praise, forever.
Praise.

(DH, 11/1/15, Psalm 111, *for Tom F.*)

SO VERY DEEP

So deep—
so very deep
is where my praise begins.
From the deepest corner
of my heart

to the greatest throng of people

I sing

of how great and tremendous God is!

God's justice booms above everything!

This God nourishes
and keeps promises.
Everything is seen and known;
everything is faithful and true,
as is everything with God.
Never ending,
forever.

God re-members us,
pulls us together
to receive a future,
enlightened by God's holy name!

When we honor God,
wisdom begins to flower.

Understanding.
Clarity.
Always.

(DH, 11/12/15, Psalm 111:1b – 3, 5 – 10)

If you seek holiness,
love God fiercely.
For then,
you will have children blest,
strong and grace-filled.

The sun will dawn on you,
with light shining,
blinding darkness,
with mercy and justice breaking through.

Charity and generosity
will be found everywhere,
fairness, integrity.

Remembered.
Yes.

Trusting in God will be
buoyant and free,
yet steady and filled with courage.
Enemies shrink:
good news—only good news.

The poor are lifted high;
righteousness prevails.
Honor discovered,
nurtured,
sustained.

Glory!

(DH, 11/4/15, Psalm 112:1b – 2, 4 – 5, 9, *For Brenna C.*)

GOD BENDS LOW

Our God bends low
to see both heaven and earth—
to raise up the weak from the dust
and to lift the poor from the ash heap,
seating them in the company of princes,
yes, with royalty and empire.

The childless are no longer alone,
rejoicing now with many children.

(DH, Psalm 113:6 – 9)

Listen,
all creatures of this earth:
Quiver!
Tremble!
Fear and honor God!

For here—
here is your promised land!
Here is your ocean of mercy,
flowing from what was once
a stubbornly hard rock!

Now,
all of our angry heat has melted!
This is the moment
when our flint edged hearts are transformed—
bubbling up like a young river!

(DH, 1/11/16, Psalm 114:7 – 8)

OPEN EYES FOR ALL TO SEE

Open eyes!
Open eyes for all to see,
but not to us, no—
not to us—
but because of your love,

impossible to name;
because of your truth,
incapable of flaws.

Why should anyone even say or think,
"Where is your God?"

Our God is without fault or excuse,
abiding, in hidden things,
and accomplishes all that is held desirable.

Our God need not answer to anyone.

For some,
their idols or "gods"
are made of hands,
measly silver and gold,
nothing special.

Because they come
from mouths that are mute,
eyes that cannot see,
ears that cannot begin to hear,
and noses completely unable
to sense the scents.

They have hands
that are unable to feel or touch,
feet that cannot make the journey,
throats that are completely silent,
with nothing to say.

They utter nothing.

And their makers—
nothing different at all;
all the same.

You who struggle,
trust the presence of the One
you cannot see—
who is our help and protection.
Let the house of Aaron and every other house,
begin to trust.

You, God,
are constantly mindful of us.

Bless us.
Bless those who struggle.
Bless the house of Aaron,
all of Israel,
and all of us who revere you.

All of us,
great and small—
may we be blessed,
blessed by the hand of the One
who fashions both heaven and earth!

God, you belong to all who live!
Here and now, on the earth!
Those who are dead cannot praise you,
nor those who have gone silent.

But for us,
for us—
we sing!

Always!
With careless abandon!
Toward all of our tomorrows!

Alleluia!

(DH, 10/14/15, Psalm 115)

I so love God...
for I have been heard.

God leans toward me
to hear my voice when I call.

Death nearly had me;
my grave was prepared,
and anguish took hold of me.
I cried out to God,
"Rescue me!"

God was and is, kind.
God was and is, faithful.
God was and is, gentle.
God protects the poor
and pulls me out of the dust.

Rest again, O my heart,
for God's love is here.
God will not let me die:
my tears will end,
and my feet will be steady.
I will know the presence of God
in this land that lives!

(DH, 9/6/15, Psalm 116:1 – 9)

God's love for me
is so deep—
hearing me,
listening to me,
when I call.

Death had me,
with traps set
grief rising,
despair increasing;
intense was my cry:
"God, free me from this!"

Compassion is God.
Gentleness is God.
Protecting poor,
raising lowly—
sleep now, rest.

Do not be afraid.
God's love is here.

My life,
is free from death,
for tears are dried;
walking steady and sure
in the path of God's walk.

Land, open and free.
Living.

(DH, 11/2/15, Psalm 116:1 – 9, *In memory of Roberta*)

Yes, I am afflicted—yet I still believe.
Yes, I am battered with lies—yet I still believe.

How can I possibly find a way
to return to God
the astonishing gift that I have been given?
I will raise the cup of liberation
and sing the name of God!
I will keep my vows to you, God,
and I will do so before your people.

God, you shed your own tears
when death comes to those
who have been faithful to you.
I beg you, God, hear me.
Here I am, your servant whom you love.
You have freed me from death.

My entire life will be a gift
of thanksgiving to you
as I call upon you, as I proclaim your name.
I will keep my vows to you, God,
and I will do so before your people—
in your house,
in the heart of your Jerusalem.

(DH, 5/20/16, Psalm 116:10 – 19, *For Alissa*)

YES, GLORY!

Praise!
From every land,
from every throat,
from the deepest heart,
from all people—
praise!

And yes, glory!
Glory to God!

The love is so strong,
so embracing,
so faithful.

Without end.
Infinite.

Now, praise that!

(DH, 12/6/15, adapt. from Psalm 117, *For Jaime*)

Praise and unending thanksgiving
be to you:
For your mercy pierces through!

Let all who struggle and suffer,
speak and celebrate:
For your mercy pierces through!

Let the house of Aaron,
and every house,
speak and celebrate:
For your mercy pierces through!

Let all who honor your name,
speak and celebrate:
For your mercy pierces through!

The nations from every corner
engulf and attempt to swallow me:
But by your name, I cut them off!

They surround me like bees
threatening to sting:
But by your name, I cut them off!

They plot to blaze up
a thorn-filled fire:
But by your name, I cut them off!

They thrust into me
deeply and with the intent of death.
But you,
     you protect me.

You are my song
that keeps me strong.
You are my song
of compassion and rescue.

(DH, 12/15/15, Psalm 118:1 – 4, 10 – 14)

Steady my stance.
Direct me.

Then, I can cast away all shame,
dwell in your presence
and linger—
taking the time I need
to follow your path.

(DH, 10/6/15, Psalm 119:5 – 6)

THE MUSIC KEEPS COMING

The music keeps coming.

When we are young,
how do we remain steady?

How do we keep our hearts
clear and clean along the way?

By living by your word,
by choosing to keep singing the song—
a song of joy
that comes from you alone.

My heart yearns for nothing,
for no one,
but you.
Keep me on track.
Do not let me wander.

The music keeps coming.

Every word of yours—I honor.
Every note that comes out of my mouth—
I will reverence as yours.
Such wisdom protects me
from poisons that can seep in and infect.

Like "ego."

It really is not that
I must "decrease"—
actually, I must "increase,"
increase and expand
my open heart
to be transformed
into becoming a "servant's heart."

You really are not trying to humble me.
I am beginning to see—
and it blows my mind—
that you are honestly,
"exalting" me—
for a higher purpose;
a holy purpose.

The music keeps coming.

I bless you
and your direction for me.

Soli Deo Gloria!
It is YOU—that I sing!

I must speak.
I cannot stay silent.
But words in and of themselves
    are shallow and empty—
    so right here,
    right now,
    I choose to SING such words;
    I choose to proudly,
    SING my faith and confidence,
    as well as my fears and doubts.

My voice,
is now—
your voice.

We are blended together.

The music keeps coming.

And with "our" voice
syncing tightly,
we become a faith-filled anthem
of unceasing rejoicing.

And rejoicing is what I need to do.
Rejoicing is what your people
are aching to do as well.

I am relentless
in singing your song,
a song that nurtures
and enriches,
bubbling over
like a faucet
that cannot be plugged.

The music keeps coming.

You honor me—
by entering and releasing from me
this most precious music.

I will go forth from this moment
to remember,
to ponder,
and to keep on choosing you.

Delight fills me.

The music keeps coming.

I give you this promise—
that I will never,
ever,
forget while I am singing—
that you are right there,
in my heart,
in my lungs,
in my breath,
in my mouth,
and on my lips
in the sound that goes forward—
and in the echo
that keeps reverberating
and returning back.

I won't forget.

Because the music keeps coming.

(DH, 1/22/16. Inspired by and grounded in Psalm 119:9 – 16,
For Abbey)

I CHERISH YOUR NAME

In the nighttime I cherish your name,
 and I honor your direction.
This means everything to me:
 to lean toward you and follow your desire.

(DH, 9/22/15, Psalm 119:55 − 56)

Infuse in me
the good sense to trust you,
to invest in your commands.

You give totally from your goodness;

show me how

I can eagerly comply and follow.

Show me comfort
through the gift of your love.

Surround and cocoon my life with tenderness,
for I take delight in your compassion.

I could never forget your wisdom,
because it keeps me alive.

I belong to you.

Bring me closer to safety,
for I will always
hold your way,
so very close.

(DH, 10/23/15, Psalm 119:66, 68, 76 – 77, 93 – 94)

I LOVE YOUR DIRECTION

O God,
I love your direction for my life:
and I contemplate it well
throughout my mind
and heart,

and throughout my day.

Your wisdom becomes my wisdom,

setting me apart,

for it is always,

always here.

You fill me with awesome insight,
beyond anything else
I have ever learned,
beyond anything
else
anyone else can provide—
because I keep your heart
close to mine.

I am determined to stay away
from false things,
and I ache to be loyal,
because you are my most blessed teacher,
my trusted guide.

I can taste the wonder of your promises,
and they are sweeter
than anything else imaginable.
I hate all that pulls me away from you.

I love your direction for my life.

(DH, 10/20/15, Psalm 119:97 – 104, *For Jimmy*)

Your word is a blazing torch
to create a path—
a light for me to follow.
My loyalty is to you.

I have suffered;
come and restore my life.
You promised.
Hear what I am crying out to you,
and teach me.

Though danger is at me from every side,
your path is never far from my heart.
Those who choose to harm me
will not deter my focus on you.
I will not stray.

Your way is my choice and destiny,
and my heart rejoices.
I am committed and determined;
I will keep saying "yes."
You are my prize.

(DH, 5/20/16, Psalm 119:105 – 112)

With a heart so full,
I ache for you to hear me.
Bring the freedom I seek
so I may follow you.

I have turned my face to you
during the cold of the night,
waiting,
praying,
to hear from you.

Throughout the night I have kept vigil,
lingering,
pondering,
musing upon your promises.

Listen to me,
you, the "God who loves;"
may I live by your justice.
Those who want to cause harm
are closing in.

But you, God,
you are even closer, so very close.
Your way shines with truth!

Since I was young,
I have learned these things about you,
and they are rooted in me forever.

(DH, 10/14/15, Psalm 119:145 – 152)

RIGHT NOW

Right now—only distress.
Right now—only anguish.
Right now—only this most lonely hour.

So I have called out to you.
You have answered.
You are present.

This is my cry,
right now:
"God, save and protect me
from those who are scheming against me!"

So, to you,
you who are scheming:
How do you think God
will reward you?
Keep sharp and look out
for the even sharper arrows
and hot coals that come your way!

Why do I have to wander
and remain such harmful places,
with those who want only violence?

I am speaking for peace.
They seem to be continually
speaking of war.

(DH, 12/15/15, Psalm 120)

The mountains hold my gaze;
it is there where I find my help.
God provides my strength.
God opens wide heaven and earth.

God will keep you steady
when you begin to stumble,
never sleeping while keeping watch.
God refuses to sleep
while holding guard over you, blessed Israel.

Protection and shade—
God provides at your right hand.
The sun will not blind your day.
The moon will not harm your night.

God will always keep you safe from harm;
your soul will be kept safe.
God will watch over your movements,
your comings and goings.

Always.

(DH, 10/10/15, adapt. Psalm 121, *for Antonio*)

I PLEDGE MYSELF

I heard them say with boundless joy,
"Let us go to God's house!"
Jerusalem—we are here inside your gates.

Jerusalem is set so perfectly
that the city and the temple are one.
It is to you, Jerusalem,
that every tribe ascends.

We are commanded to honor the name of God.
The places of righteousness and justice are here,
in line with the glory of David.

For Jerusalem—pray for peace.
For Jerusalem—pray for happiness in every home.
For Jerusalem—pray for safety in their walls.
For Jerusalem—pray for peace in every dwelling.

For love of my family and friends,
let me sing, "Peace!"

For love of God's own house,
I pledge myself
and pray seeking goodness -
for you.

(DH, 10/28/15, Psalm 122)

Our eyes sink into your presence,
totally fixed on you.

Our eyes want to stay on you—
gaze on you,
always seeking you,
searching you,
longing for you.

Our eyes are so focused on you,
like a slave following his master,
like a servant loyal to her mistress;
we will not deter from you;
we are waiting for your mercy.

Keep showing your mercy to us,
for we have suffered so much,
and we are desperate for relief
from the mockery we receive;
and from the shame
that is thrust upon us.

(DH, 1/11/16, Psalm 123)

We are now, souls —rescued,
    like birds fleeing the hunter.

If God had not stayed with us,
if God had not been with us and for us—
then we would have been eaten alive,
destroyed by the heat, anger, and rage
of those who hate us.

We would have drowned
from the waters in their tempest,
the surge of the waves
would have consumed us,
overwhelmed us.

But God came
and broke open the trapper's net—
the snare is broken.
We are set free.

God is our help—
the creator of earth and sky.

(DH, 12/28/15, Psalm 124)

Let go.

Trust in God,
and be like Zion—
strong, unmovable, enduring.

Just as the mountains surround us,
let God embrace you
day after day,
from tomorrow to tomorrow.

Unending.
Let God ring you in.

Keep close to the border of righteousness.
Keep wrong choices
and misguided directions at bay.
It gets slippery.

So God,
bring your goodness
to the good ones.
Bring your justice
to the just ones.
Bring your truth
to the ones whose hearts are true.
The cruel and the evil
will continue to bring their poison.
Cast these powers away!

Give us peace.
A peace that lasts.

(DH, 12/4/15, Psalm 125)

You bring us out of our cell,
our "locked in" place.

The dreaming is now set free!
Laughter now replaces our tears!
Dancing arrives to our crippled legs!
Songs return to our silent lips!

Others now say:

"Yes!
Look at them!
God is with them!
Wonderful things are happening
to those who have struggled—
     God is the reason!
Rejoice in this!"

God,
share with us the same drink
that they are consuming—
we too, thirst—
we ache to be drunk with the water
that can cover the dry ground.

May our tears
be the fountain that nurtures
and brings back
singing, dancing, and laughing.

They once left weeping and grieving,
and they planted the seed.
Now, they come back—
and we want to join them
in their song, dance, and joy!

(DH, 4/15/16, Psalm 126, *for Jamie*)

If God is not the one
building my house,
the work will be useless –
it will fall.
If God is not keeping watch,
those who stand guard—
will watch and stand by in vain.

If we rise early
and work and sweat all day for bread,
we are foolish.
If God is pleased,
we will all receive,
even when we are at rest.

Children are a most blessed gift from God,
and a precious blessing
for those who bear them.
They are like the arrows of the archer.

So very happy and grateful
are those whose quiver is full—
they will bear no reason to be ashamed
when facing their foes.

(DH, 12/15/15, Psalm 127)

We are full of happiness and bliss;
in awe,
standing in your presence.

How rich is your table,
the bounty of your hands!
Your beloved one
is like the vine bearing rich fruit
warm from your presence.

Children circle 'round this table,
like olive saplings—
such a blessing they are!
Blessings abound
when we honor God.

May we know God's blessing
and receive the gift
of such precious happiness.
May Jerusalem,
and may all of us,
live to see our grandchildren.

And one day—
in our journey of questions and struggle,
may we know the peace
that comes from God above.

(DH, 1/11/16, Psalm 128, *For Doug and Brenna*)

We may receive
cruel wounds,
but in the end,
their words and actions
will fail
when in the presence
of God's justice.

(DH, 1/11/16, Psalm 129:1 – 2)

Right now,
at this very moment—
I feel so empty.
I need to grab on to something,
I need to know
that you are not cutting me off.
I need to know that you are listening.
Hear me!

I am begging you,
please have mercy on me,
because if you were to keep count
of all my sins,
of all my horrible deeds,
I would not be able to survive
your judgment.

But you do forgive.
You keep on forgiving me.
I trust in that—
I trust in you.
I wait and keep watch for you.

I am one with everyone
who is waiting for you.
I will wait,
and I know you will fill me
with grace,
with mercy—
and I will be free from my sin.

(DH, 12/7/15, Psalm 130)

PEACE

You: peace.

Not haughty,
not arrogant,
not reaching beyond myself.

You: peace.

But yes, calm.
Still.
Like a child
sinking—
surrendering to mother.

Rest.

You: peace.

Everyone,
wait for God.
Always.

You: peace.

(DH, 11/3/15, Psalm 131)

God has chosen Zion.
God has chosen all of us
and desires us
to have this sacred home.

God has chosen our hearts
for this home,
an everlasting dwelling place.

This home
will be blessed with abundance—
especially for the poor.
All who serve
will be cloaked in holiness,
and the faithful
will end up singing and singing!

This home
is the center of strength
for the power of light
for God's anointed.
Those who oppose this gift,
will be covered in shame.
But God's anointed
will receive a crown bearing light!

(DH, 1/11/16, Psalm 132:13 – 18)

WHEN WE ARE TETHERED

How so very good.
How wonderful!
When we are tethered
and intimate together—
as one life.

Together.

It is like warm oil
massaging the head,
dripping down the cheek,
sliding under the collar.

It is like the dew
when it serenely flows
down the mountain.

It is like this,
there and then—
when life shines.

Life together.
Always.

(DH, 12/2/15, Psalm 133, *For HH*)

Bless God,
and all who serve in God's house.
Bless all
who keep watch throughout the night.

Lift up your hands in the holy place,
and bless God.

And may God,
who designs the entirety of the earth
and the infinite vastness of the sky,
bless you, always,
from Zion.

(DH, 8/7/15, Psalm 134)

GIVE PRAISE!

Alleluia!

Give praise to the name of God,
give praise,
give praise,
keep on giving praise!

All of you who have a servant's heart—
give praise!

All of you who stand in God's presence—
give praise!

All of you who long to sing
a hymn of thanksgiving to God—
give praise!

Israel, every nation—
give praise!

God is great indeed,
and surpasses every gift,
over and over again.

If God wants it so—
it will be so!
No matter what,
and no matter where:
in heaven,
on the earth,
or in the sea.

God adorns the earth with clouds,
and never hesitates
to burst forth lightning for the rain,
or to release the brilliant breath of life!

May every home give praise!

Alleluia!

(DH, 1/11/16, Psalm 135:1 – 7, 19 – 21, *For Baboo*)

ISRAEL, BLESS GOD!

Your name is relentless—it is forever.
Your glory never fades—it is forever.
You are justice for your people,
and you are attentive to their needs.

The things of gold and silver
are the idols of human hands.
Their mouths cannot make a sound.
Their eyes see nothing.
Their ears cannot hear anything.
Their nostrils cannot find air to breathe.

Israel—bless God!
House of Aaron,
House of Levi—bless God!
All who are faithful—bless God!

Bless the God of Zion,
who calls Jerusalem home.

(DH, 12/20/15, Psalm 135:13 – 21)

God's love is unending!

God is good, the God of Gods!
God's love is unending!

God is the creator of all worlds!
God's love is unending!

God is the designer of the skies!
God's love is unending!

God laid out the land on the sea!
God's love is unending!

God turned on the great lights!
God's love is unending!

God welcomed the sun!
God's love is unending!

God brought forth the stars, the moon, the
darkness!
God's love is unending!

God is our escape from bondage, by the arm of
power!
God's love is unending!

God split the sea in two!
God's love is unending!

God let Israel cross over!
God's love is unending!

God drowned Pharaoh and his armies!
God's love is unending!

God led us through the desert!
God's love is unending!

God neutralized the enemy tribes and conquered
the evil monarchs!
God's love is unending!

God gave Israel a beautiful land!
God's love is unending!

God never forgot our suffering!
God's love is unending!

God always brings a victory!
God's love is unending!

God sustains all living things!
God's love is unending!

God be given thanks in the highest heaven!
God's love is unending!

(DH, 1/11/16, Psalm 136, *For Paki*)

Weeping, weeping,
    remembering Zion.

The willows were bent low—
    there we hung our harps.

In our exile,
we were tormented and shamed
into singing
    "happy songs of Zion."

Sarcasm.
Humiliation.

How could we possibly
sing such songs
    in such a place,
so foreign to our well being?

Forget Jerusalem?
Forget God's people?
Never.
Let my hand be paralyzed
and fall off
instead of losing my memory!
May my voice be silenced,
if I forget to turn back toward you,
and celebrate my joy.

Babylon—be doomed!
May you be covered in cursing
for what you have done!

You deserve evil for evil.
May good rest upon those
who have smashed your children
upon the rocks.

(DH, 1/11/16, Psalm 137:1 – 6, 8)

I thank you, God,
with all that I am.

I join the music of heaven
to praise your name,
for you have listened to the poor,
and you increase their strength.

The moment I call out—
you respond.

No hesitation.

You sit high—
but you look low,
always loving.

Whether you are very close
or far away,
you always seem to know...
yes, you always know.

When I am afraid,
you keep me breathing;
you keep me alive.

You lift me up with your hand,
rescue-filled.

My cause becomes your cause.

My need for your love
is always satisfied.

Stay,
please stay,
do not leave what you have created.

Keep listening,

Stay.

(DH, 1/11/16, Psalm 138:1 – 2, 6 – 8, *For Lou Anne*)

You know me.
Your beam goes right through me:
and sees everything,
understands everything,
finds everything –
and knows.

Everything.

When I sit,
when I stand,
all my thoughts—
before they even begin
to arrive in my mind—
you have knowledge of it all.

Even before I attempt to speak,
you know it already
and you speak it.
You are behind, before,
with your gentle hand
calmly touching me—

or may be planning to go.

It is impossible for my mind
and my heart
to wrap around this mystery.
It is incomprehensible.
I cannot begin to grasp it.

Where could I possibly go to escape you?
How could I even imagine fleeing from you,
and remove myself from your presence?

If I ascend toward heaven—there you are.
If I descend to the bottom of this world—there you
are.
Your grip and hold on me
is everywhere,
in every way:
if I fly toward the rising of the morning;
if I go down to the depths of the sea,
you are there.

You are there.

Every part of me—
you created
and you placed me
in the warm waters
of my mother's womb.
What a wonder this is!
My gratitude is bursting.

You have embroidered me
into your fabric—
I am your material;
your garment in this physical world.

You have recorded
and kept record
of my every moment,
long before such moments
could be imagined.

Your thoughts—
so treasured and precious!
Their depth,
beyond anything I could ever know.

You know me so well.
Actually,
you know me too well.

(DH, 1/5/16, Psalm 139:1 – 10, 13 – 18, *For Lori*)

I KNOW MY GOD

I know my God.
I know how God will act.
The weak and the poor
will be held tight to God's side.

God is deserving
of all the honor I can muster,
of all the praise I can give,
because the innocent live on,
always in God's sight.

(DH, 1/11/16, Psalm 140:13 – 14)

My cry to you is urgent.

So I beg you,
do not delay in answering my call.
My prayer is rising before you now
like the burning of incense;
my hands are lifted high,
as a most serious evening oblation.

Place a guard over my mouth,
like a sentry at the door of my lips.
May evil words never sound forth from me;
may I never consider or choose
anything hateful or cruel.
May I keep my distance
from the wicked;
and never linger at their table.

If someone just corrects me,
may I be humble enough
to receive it as a gracious kindness.
But may I never
receive an anointing
from evil sources;
I pray that I will resist.

God, I turn myself totally toward you,
for I only seek you for safety.
Keep me alive.
Do not trick me with traps
that may be set before me.
Let my foes receive their own fate.
But please,
help me to escape their lost destiny.

(DH, 1/11/16, Psalm 141:1 – 5, 8 – 10)

I am praying,
O dear God,
I am praying.
I am being hunted down,
and feel deserted by everyone.

I am surrendering my troubles;
here they are,
dripping down before you.
My breath
is getting shorter and shorter,
more faint,
as I keep walking on this road
filled with traps
that are hidden everywhere.

Can you not see what is happening here?
No one seems to be my friend right now.

I have nowhere else to turn,
for I see no escape.
So I am turning to you,
my only route and path
to a land that is living.

Can you not hear me?
I am going hoarse
as I cry out to you.
Listen to me!
Rescue me!

I feel my foes closing in,
and I am frozen by my fear.

Set me free from this box!
For my freedom,
I will sing endlessly,
for I will most certainly know
that you are the one
who gave me back my life.

(DH, 1/11/16, Psalm 142)

IN YOU ALONE

May I,
this morning,
be an announcement

of your love,
for it is in you alone

that I place my trust.

Show me

and guide me in ways that are right.

I offer you myself

Everything I have.

Everything I am.

(DH, 9/5/15, Psalm 143:8, *For Mark T.*)

Praise and blessing!
You, my rock!

You, strength for the conflict.
You, my hands for the challenge.

You, my wall of safety.

You, my castle.

You, my deepest love.

You, my victory.

How is it that you always care for us?
How is it that you always give more
than just the time of day?
We are a mere breath,
a puff of smoke,
    and our days are like passing shadows.

Bend the sky downward,
and touch the mountains—
caress them until they explode into flames!
Strike the lightning and thunderbolts,
and let the arrows soar!
Pluck me out from the terror of the waters
and the grip of the strangers
who seduce by their lies.

A brand new and vibrant song
I will sing for you—
I will strum and play my praises,
for yours is the music of finishing first;
you rescue David from the sword.

You mold your sons and daughters
like the plants that grow vigorously,
and the cornerstones that are dug deep.

You feed our barns to the full
with endless grain;
the sheep bless our fields,
and the oxen are numerous and strong.

Protection is strong.
There is no breaking in or breaking out—
no shouting in the streets.

Happy are all of us who live like this!
Happy are all of us who give our lives to you,
fully and without reserve!

We are blest!

(DH, 12/2/15, Psalm 144, *For Anna*)

Every day,
every moment,
every thought,
every action—
all give praise!

No end in sight,

only beginning

again and again.

Always new.

"Always great" is who
and what you are—
what you always do.

Too infinite to capture,
too amazing,
too deep.

The stories of praising you
are passed down
and down—
singing splendor;
glorious majesty;
works of wonder!

Everything is percolating,
exposing gratitude;
transformed into blessing,
a most faithful blessing;
singing of your city of justice,
and the wisdom of your ways.

(DH, 11/7/15, Psalm 145: 2-3, 4-5, 10-11, *For Cameron*)

Everyone and everything—praise!
Creation, give praise!
Faithful ones, give praise!
Blessings, give praise!
Glory upon Glory, give praise!

All things and creatures

give witness—

declare, proclaim!

God is faithful.
God is gracious.
God is holy.
God is "always there."

Present.

Lifting up fallen ones,
raising up lowly ones.
God, we all look to you,
and you feed us when it is time.
Your hands, always open,
answering and responding,
filling our desire.

You keep us alive!

May the singing never end,
may the praising never end,
may the blessing never end,
tomorrow and beyond!

Always:
that means, "forever!"

(DH, 10/27/15, Psalm 145:10 – 11, 13c – 16, 19 – 21)

God,
I hold you high above all things in my heart.
Everywhere and always,
each and every day
I will be a song of blessing to you.

You are great and large,
and your greatness and goodness
are beyond anything I can put into words.
Any level of praise sounded to you
will always fall short,
never enough.

Every age yearns to sing your story
over and over again.

Endless.

I will take a stand
and announce your actions.
My acclamation of praise
will weave together your goodness
and your justice.

You are gracious.
You are compassionate.
Kindness overflowing;
tender mercies always moving.

Everything is drenched
in thanksgiving for you,
and for the brightness of your presence.

Generation after generation
join in the glorious praise of you—

in your acts that are so decisive,
in your strength that is so firm,
in your pattern that weaves through everything
and anything.

You hold up those who fall.
You raise up those who are beaten down.

God's justice stirs and seeps into
places unseen,
and is found in the crying out—
feeding the living.

God is just in every way imaginable,
with love surrounding everything.
God is near to everyone who cries out.
close by all whose hearts ache.

God keeps promises—
always listening, always protecting.

Those who love God are preserved,
and kept holy and alive.
God keeps hanging on to us.
Those who abandon God
are only abandoning themselves.

Everywhere and always,
this blessing of God will sing out—
full of holy praise.

(DH, 9/2/15, Psalm 145, *For Lia and Lindsey*)

GOD IS FOREVER

Every part of me,
my soul,
my body,
every inch of me
wants to honor and praise God,
as long as I can,
as long as will live.

It is not wise
to lay your trust
with mere human leaders—
they will disappoint!
Once they die,
their promises decay.
But with God—
all moves on,
the future is secure!

It is very wise
to trust God's vision,
for God is the maker of everything,
and always keeps faith with us!

God is food for the starving,
justice for the poor and hopeless,
freedom for those held captive.

Eyes are opened!
Limbs that are bent
are made straight!
Widows and orphans
are no longer alone!
Strangers are welcomed;
no longer aliens!

God,
give out love
to those who live justice;
and subvert all
who deprive
anyone of dignity.

Praise God!
God is forever!
So likewise,
our praise is forever!

Life leads to more life!

(DH, 1/11/16, Psalm 146:1 – 4, 6b – 10)

It is so good!
Sing it!

It is so good
to praise,

to give thanks

to this God of ours

who makes no distinctions

in pouring out mercy.

God rebuilds us,
restores us,
gathers
and regathers us,
over and over again—
and never gets tired
of lavishing us with mercy.

Broken hearts are healed.
Our wounds are attended to,
and wrapped in love.
Every star is given a name—
and so are we.
We are so unbelievably
known by God,
who keeps calling us
by the dignity of our names.

God's power is endless,
God's wisdom reaches above
and visits us,
fills us,
and changes us.

When we are bent over,
you help us to stand tall—
you strengthen and sustain.

(DH, 12/5/15, Psalm 147:1 – 6a)

LISTEN WELL

Listen well, Jerusalem!
Zion, be attentive, and praise!

God has kept you safe,
for you are locked in and protected;
provided with children,

peaceful in your homes,

and fed well with the finest of wheat.

God continues to speak:
Word proclaimed, spoken, shouted!
    Snow sprinkles down like diamonds;
    frost sows like the dust,
    and is scattered about,
    and flees away by the melting wind.

God speaks the Word;
to all of you, the direction is given.
You alone, O Jacob,
are the landing point and target
for God's voice.

No one else can hear!

(DH, 10/29/15, Psalm 147:12 – 16, 19 – 20)

Praise God with beauty unspeakable!
Praise God from the crown of the mountain!
All angels, praise!
All heavenly hosts, praise!

The brightness of the sun,
the brilliance of the moon,
the sparkle of the stars,
the splash of the rain,
the thrill of heaven,
the heat of the fire,
the depths of the depths,
the creatures that crawl and swim,
the rush of the waters—
all offer up your praise!

All people, royal and common!
All who judge and all who follow!

Women and men,
young and old,
offer up the name in praise—
the name that drowns out
all other names!

Beyond words, praise be given!
All that is life—praise!
All that is and can be created—praise!
From our yesterdays through our tomorrows,
—may all laws be celebrated inside and outside!

God's people be strong!
God's faithful shout praise!
Rise up all children of Israel—
   all sing and be praise!

(DH, 10/17/15, Psalm 148, *For Mom*)

Sing!
Come on, sing!
Not just any song,
but a NEW song—
a YOUNG song.

If you are among God's faithful,

then sing!

But be sure, however,
to not sing alone:
sing with each other,
with everyone gathered!

Find more if possible,

find as many as you can
to join you in your song!

If they do not know how—
then teach them.

Israel—sing!
Zion—sing!

And along with your singing—
dance!
Dance in the name of God,
with instruments of all kinds
driving the rhythm!

Why?

Because our God
delights and revels in us—
all of us,
broken and in need of saving.

Every community,
every family—
join in.
As loudly as you can—
then nothing can defeat you!

Nothing.

Come on, you faithful ones,
sing!
This is your promise,
your glory!
There is no better response!

Alleluia!

(DH, 12/4/15, Psalm 149, *For Ryan*)

You!

Praise You!
You in your home!
You in the heavens!

You!

Strong!
Holy!
Deeds upon deeds!

You!

Power from the trumpets!
Glory from the many strings!
Harps with glissandos!
Justice dancing!
Drums pounding!
Timbrels clanging!
Pipes blasting!

You!

Joy from crashing cymbals!
Ecstasy from ringing!
Endless bell overtones!
Everything resonating!
Everything breathing fully and clearly!
Everything alive!

You!

(DH, 11/29/15, Psalm 150, *For Kevin*)

Indexes

PSALMS

PRAYER AND SPECIAL NEEDS

Anger:
Psalms 10, 13, 22, 58, 69, 73, 77

At the Time of Death:
Psalms 22, 23, 91, 131

Being at Peace:
Psalms 4, 16, 29, 62, 85, 112, 122, 131, 134

Called to Justice:
Psalms 11, 14, 15, 18, 20, 25, 40, 45, 53, 68 69, 72, 85, 97, 99, 101, 112, 113, 119

Calm:
Psalms 16, 23, 27, 36, 40, 56, 64, 77, 107, 124

Celebrating God's Word:
Psalms 13, 19, 95, 130, 147

Celebrating Life:
Psalms 9, 29, 33, 34, 47, 66, 84, 108, 148, 150

Clear Thinking:
Psalms 4, 11, 32, 40, 95, 97, 131

Closeness to God:
Psalms 4, 12, 16, 19, 24, 25, 27, 30, 33, 36, 62, 130, 139

Community: the "Body of Christ"
Psalms 15, 33, 68, 100, 101, 108, 122, 126, 128, 133

In Times of Fear:
Psalm 3, 4, 6, 7, 10, 13, 21, 22, 23, 27, 28, 34, 38, 54, 55, 56, 57, 59, 64, 70, 77, 90, 91, 102, 121, 142

In Times of Need:
Psalms 3, 4, 5, 6, 10, 13, 16, 17, 24, 26, 28, 30, 31, 32, 35, 39, 42-43, 51, 55, 56, 57, 61, 64, 69, 70, 83, 85, 88, 90, 91, 102, 109, 123, 234, 142

In Times of Pain:
Psalms 7, 10, 12, 13, 31, 32, 34, 39, 57, 69, 77, 102, 109, 121, 123

In Times of Stress:
Psalms 3, 6, 7, 22, 23, 26, 28, 31, 32, 39, 42-43, 56, 59, 61, 64, 83, 88, 91, 102, 121, 131, 142

In Times of Trouble:
Psalms 3, 5, 6, 7, 12, 13, 22, 23, 31, 32, 39, 41, 55, 57, 62, 64, 70, 77, 83, 91, 123, 132, 142, 143

In Times of Loneliness:
Psalms 13, 22, 56, 69, 77, 88, 01, 102, 121

Letting Go of Guilt and Shame:
Psalms 23, 31, 32, 38, 41, 71, 103, 123

Letting Go of Perfection:
Psalms 30, 40, 51, 139

Listening to God:
Psalms 5, 16, 42-43, 63, 95, 131, 143, 144

Meditation:
Psalms 8, 23, 42-43, 131, 139

Ministry and Service:
Psalms 15, 20, 40, 68, 72, 97, 101, 113, 116, 117

Moving Forward in Life:
Psalms 16, 19, 20, 40, 51, 95, 97, 104, 118, 119, 122, 126, 138, 144, 148, 149

My Gifts and the Gifts of Others:
Psalms 19, 20, 34, 36, 40, 72, 84, 103, 111

New Beginnings:
Psalms 8, 12, 16, 24, 26, 36, 40, 56, 84, 97, 104, 108, 117, 118, 126, 139, 147

Openness to God:
Psalms 4, 16, 19, 23, 24, 31, 63, 81, 95, 116, 119, 124, 134

Patience:
Psalms 13, 33, 127

Praising God:
Psalms 8, 9, 18, 29, 33, 34, 47, 48, 66, 67, 71, 81, 86, 96, 97, 99, 105, 108, 113, 118, 124, 126, 135, 136, 144, 145, 147, 148, 149, 150

Praying for Others:
Psalms 100, 103, 104, 112, 117, 121, 122, 148, 150

Recovery and Renewal:
Psalms 22, 23, 27, 31, 32, 33, 40, 41, 42-43, 51, 54, 55, 56, 57, 62, 70, 71, 91, 103, 111, 121, 122, 126, 130, 140

Resurrection:
Psalms 47, 66, 98, 104, 105, 118, 126, 136, 147, 149, 150

Safety:
Psalms 3, 7, 11, 12, 16, 20, 23, 26, 27, 30, 31, 37, 41, 54, 56, 57, 62, 70, 76, 84, 91, 103, 107, 121, 140

Seeking and Speaking the Truth:
Psalms 20, 24, 26, 34, 36, 50, 101, 121, 136

Seeking Comfort:
Psalms 223, 27, 31, 36, 41, 56, 59, 70, 86, 89, 90, 91, 111, 121, 124, 139, 142

Seeking God's Guidance:
Psalms 15, 16, 19, 20, 23, 24, 25, 26, 36, 40, 69, 80, 95, 100, 101, 11, 132, 137

Struggling with Integrity:
Psalms 12, 15, 19, 26, 50, 57, 68, 85, 101, 103, 109

LITURGICAL, SEASONAL, SOLEMNITIES AND FEASTS

Advent:
Psalms 24, 25, 72, 80, 85, 89, 122, 126, 146

The Immaculate Conception of the Blessed Virgin Mary:
Psalm 98

Christmas:
Psalms 80, 89, 96, 97, 128

The Holy Family of Jesus, Mary, and Joseph:
Psalm 84, 105, 128

The Blessed Virgin Mary, Mother of God:
Psalm 67

Epiphany:
Psalm 72

Baptism of the Lord:
Psalm 29, 104,

The Presentation of the Lord:
Psalm 24

Ash Wednesday:
Psalm 51

Lent:
Psalms 19, 23, 25, 27, 32, 33, 51, 91, 95, 103, 116, 126, 130, 137

St. Joseph, Husband of the Blessed Virgin Mary:
Psalm 89

The Annunciation of the Lord:
Psalm 40

Palm Sunday:
Psalm 22

Holy Thursday:
Psalm 116

Good Friday:
Psalm 22, 31

Easter Vigil:
Psalms 16, 19, 30, 33, 42-43, 51, 104, 118

Easter Sunday:
Psalms 66, 118, 136

Easter Season:
Psalms 4, 16, 23, 27, 30, 33, 66, 67, 97, 98, 100, 118, 136, 145, 150

Ascension:
Psalm 47

Pentecost:
Psalm 104

The Most Holy Trinity:
Psalms 8, 33

The Most Holy Body and Blood of Christ (Corpus Christi):
Psalm 116

The Most Sacred Heart of Jesus:
Psalm 23, 103

The Nativity of St. John the Baptist
Psalms 71, 139

Saints Peter and Paul, Apostles:
Psalms, 19, 34

The Transfiguration of the Lord:
Psalm 97

The Assumption of the Blessed Virgin Mary:
Psalms 45, 132

The Exaltation of the Cross:
Psalm 78

All Saints:
Psalm 24

All Souls / The Commemoration of All the Faithful Departed:
Psalms 23, 25, 103, 116, 130,

The Dedication of the Lateran Basilica:
Psalm 46

Christ the King:
Psalms 23, 122

The Immaculate Conception of the
Blessed Virgin Mary:
Psalm 98

SACRAMENTS AND OTHER RITUALS

Baptism / Christian Initiation /
Confirmation:
Psalms 22, 23, 27, 29, 33, 34, 66, 98,
104, 105, 117, 118, 136, 145

Reconciliation:
Psalms 8, 13, 23, 25, 27, 31, 32, 33, 36,
51, 85, 95, 103, 123, 139, 145

Marriage:
Psalms 8, 16, 33, 34, 103, 112, 128,
145, 148

Anointing of the Sick:
Psalms 6, 23, 25, 27, 29, 34, 42, 43,
51, 63, 71, 84, 85, 86, 103, 123, 145

Celebrations of Ministry (Ordinations,
Religious Professions):

Psalms 16, 23, 40, 84, 89, 96, 100,
116, 117

Funerals / Masses for the Dead:
Psalms 23, 25, 27, 29, 42, 43, 51, 63,
103, 116, 121, 122, 123, 126, 130

Morning Prayer:
Psalms 5, 19, 24, 33, 42, 51, 57, 63, 84,
85, 90, 97, 98, 118

Evening Prayer:
Psalms 16, 27, 30, 45, 46, 116, 123,
132, 145

Night Prayer: 23, 25, 31, 103

CALENDAR: FEAST DAYS OF SAINTS /
PROPHETS AND WITNESSES /
SPECIAL CELEBRATIONS AND OCCASIONS

JANUARY

January 2
SS. Basil the Great &
Gregory Nazianzen:
Psalm 23

January 4
St. Elizabeth Ann Seton:
Psalms 1, 15, 16,

January 5
St. John Neumann:
Psalm 145

January 6
St. André Bessette:
Psalm 27

January 7
St. Raymond of
Penyafort:
Psalm 103

January 7
Galileo Galilei:
Psalm 8, 148

January 13
St. Hilary:
Psalm 110

January 15
Martin Luther King, Jr.:
Psalms 33, 71, 133,

January 17
St. Anthony:
Psalm 16

January 20
St. Fabian:
Psalm 40

January 20
St. Sebastian:
Psalm 34

January 21
St. Agnes:
Psalm 23

January 22
St. Vincent:
Psalm 34

January 23
St. Marianne Cope:
Psalm 113

January 24
St. Francis de Sales:
Psalm 37

January 25
The Conversion of
St. Paul:
Psalm 117

January 26
SS. Timothy and Titus
Psalm 96

January 27
St. Angela Merici:
Psalm 148

January 28
St. Thomas Aquinas:
Psalm 119

January 30
Mahatma Gandhi:
Psalm 15, 29

January 31
St. John Bosco:
Psalm 103

FEBRUARY

Black History Month:
Psalm 34, 43, 56, 107

February 1
St. Brigid of Kildare:
Psalm 42

February 2
St. Cornelius
Psalm 87

February 3
St. Blaise:
Psalm 117

February 3
Simeon:
Psalm 112

February 3
St. Ansgar:
Psalm 96

February 5
St. Agatha:
Psalm 31

February 5
Pedro Arrupe
Psalm 145

February 6
St. Paul Miki and his
Companions:
Psalm 126

February 8
St. Jerome Emiliani:
Psalm 34

February 10
St. Scholastica:
Psalm 148

February 11
Our Lady of Lourdes:
Canticle of Judith

February 12
St. Julian the Hospitaller:
Psalms 90, 136

February 12
Sr. Dorothy Stang,
SNDdeN:
Psalms 15, 33, 65, 113

February 14
SS. Cyril and Methodius:
Psalm 117

February 15
Ben Salmon:
Psalm 29

February 17
The Seven Holy Founders
of the Servite Order:
Psalm 34

February 19
Asian American Heritage
Day:
Psalms 18, 108

February 20
Henri de Lubac, SJ
Psalm 149

February 21
St. Peter Damian:
Psalm 16

February 21
John Henry Newman
Psalm 123

February 22
The Chair of St. Peter:
Psalm 23

February 23
St. Polycarp:
Psalm 31

February 26
St. Photini,
The Samaritan Woman:
Psalm 95

April 10
Pierre Teilhard de
Chardin:
Psalms 65, 150

April 11
St. Stanislaus:
Psalm 34

April 13
St. Martin I:
Psalm 126

April 15
Abraham Lincoln:
Psalm 15

April 16
St. Benedict Joseph
Labré:
Psalm 33

April 21
St. Anselm:
Psalm 34

April 22
Earth Day:
Psalms 19, 33, 65, 104

April 23
St. George:
Psalm 126

April 23
St. Adalbert:
Psalm 31

April 23
Cesar Chavez:
Psalms 56, 73, 135

April 24:
St. Fidelis of Sigmar-
ingen:
Psalm 34

April 25
St. Mark:
Psalm 89

April 26
William Stringfellow:
Psalm 128

April 26
Lesbian Visibility Day:
Psalms 5, 33, 90, 113,
126, 146

April 27
St. Zita:
Psalms 42, 122, 123

April 28
St. Peter Chanel:
Psalm 117

April 28
St. Louis Mary de
Montfort:
Psalm 40

April 29
St. Catherine of Siena:
Psalm 103

April 30
St. Pius V:
Psalm 110

April 30
St. Marie of the
Incarnation:
Psalm 62

MAY

May 1
St. Joseph the Worker:
Psalm 90

May 2
St. Athanasius:
Psalm 37

May 3
SS. Philip and James:
Psalm 19

May 4
St. Florian:
Psalm 16

May 9
Blessed Theresa
Gerhardinger:
Psalm 103

May 9
Isaiah:
Psalm 112

May 10
St. Damien of Molokai:
Psalm 68

May 10
Karl Barth:
Psalm 112

May 11
Solomon:
Psalms 8, 72

May 12
Sts. Nereus and
Achilleus:
Psalm 124

May 12
St. Pancras:
Psalm 103

May 13
Blessed Julian of
Norwich:
Psalm 8, 112

May 14
St. Matthias:
Psalm 113

May 14
St. Mother Theodore
Guerin
Psalm 34, 116

The Second Sunday in May
Peace of the Home;
Shalom Bayit
(To replace Mother's
Day and Father's Day,
during the months of
May and June):
Psalms 15, 84, 91

May 15
St. Isidore:
Psalm 1, 65

May 15
St. Dymphna:
Psalms 62, 131

May 16
Peter Maurin:
Psalm 117

May 18
St. John I:
Psalm 23

May 20
St. Bernardine of Siena:
Psalm 40

May 24
Job:
Psalm 22, 31, 137

May 25
St. Bede the Venerable:
Psalm 119

May 25
St. Gregory VII:
Psalm 110

May 25
St. Mary Magdalene de'
Pazzi:
Psalm 148

May 27
St. Augustine of
Canterbury:
Psalm 96

May 30
St. Joan of Arc
Psalms 15, 113

May 31
The Visitation of the
Blessed Virgin Mary /
Mary and Martha
Psalms 128, 145

JUNE

LGBT Pride Month:
Psalms 5, 33, 90, 113,
126, 146

June 1
St. Justin:
Psalm 34

June 1
National Day for the
Protection of Children:
Psalm 131

June 2
SS. Marcellinus and Peter:
Psalm 124

June 2
National Gun Violence
Awareness Day
Psalms 91, 129, 131

June 3
St. Charles Lwanga and
Companions:
Psalm 124

June 5
St. Boniface:
Psalm 117

June 7
Chief Seattle
Psalm 33

June 6
St. Norbert:
Psalm 23

June 9
St. Ephrem:
Psalm 37

June 11
St. Barnabas:
Psalm 98

June 12
Anne Frank:
Psalms 23, 42

June 13
St. Anthony of Padua:
Psalm 89

June 15
St. Vitus:
Psalm 150

June 15
The Prophet Amos
Psalm 15, 113

June 19
St. Romuald:
Psalm 131

June 21
St. Aloysius Gonzaga:
Psalm 16

June 22
St. Paulinus of Nola:
Psalm 40

June 22
St. Thomas More:
Psalm 23

June 22
SS. John Fisher and
Thomas More:
Psalm 126

June 24
The Nativity of St. John
the Baptist:
Psalms 71, 139

June 26
Virgil Michael:
Psalm 116

June 27
St. Cyril of Alexandria:
Psalm 89

June 27
Helen Keller:
Psalm 123

June 28
St. Irenaeus:
Psalm 37

June 29
SS. Peter and Paul:
Psalms 19, 34

June 29
The Gifts of Sexuality
and Gender:
Psalm 16, 63, 139

June 30
The First Martyrs of the
Holy Roman Church:
Psalm 124

JULY

July 1
St. Junipero Serra:
Psalm 128

July 3
St. Thomas the Apostle:
Psalm 117

July 4
St. Elizabeth of Portugal:
Psalm 112

July 4
Independence Day:
Seeking Liberty and
Justice for All
Psalms 40, 50, 72, 85

July 5
St. Anthony Mary
Zaccaria:
Psalm 1

July 6
St. Maria Goretti:
Psalm 31

July 7
The Prophet Isaiah:
Psalm 112

July 11
St. Benedict:
Psalm 34

July 13
St. Henry:
Psalm 1

July 14
St. Kateri Tekakwitha:
Psalm 100

July 13
Silas
Psalms 146, 148, 149

July 15
St. Bonaventure:
Psalm 119

July 16
Our Lady of Mt. Carmel:
Psalm 29, 45

July 18
St. Camillus de Lellis:
Psalm 1

July 21
St. Lawrence of Brindisi:
Psalm 40

July 21
The Prophet Daniel:
Psalm 136

July 22
St. Mary Magdalene:
Psalm 63

July 23
St. Bridget of Sweden:
Psalm 34

July 23
The Prophet Ezekiel
Psalm 149

July 25
St. James, Apostle:
Psalm 126

July 26
SS. Joachim and Anne:
Psalm 132

July 29
St. Martha:
Psalm 34

July 29
William Wilberforce
Psalm 91

July 30
St. Peter Chrysologus:
Psalm 119

July 31
St. Ignatius of Loyola:
Psalm 34

AUGUST

August 1
St. Alphonsus Liguori:
Psalm 119

August 2
St. Eusebius of Vercelli:
Psalm 89

St. Peter Julian Eymard:
Psalm 34

August 4
St. John Mary Vianney:
Psalm 117

August 6
Transfiguration of the Lord:
Psalm 97

SEPTEMBER

September 16
St. Cornelius:
Psalm 126

September 17
St. Robert Bellarmine:
Psalm 19

September 19
St. Januarius:
Psalm 126

September 20
Sts. Andrew Kim Tae-gon
and Paul Chong Ha-sang,
and Companions:
Psalm 126

September 21
St. Matthew:
Psalm 19

September 21
St. Teresa of Calcutta
Psalms 11, 34, 128,
119, 131

September 21
Jonah:
Psalm 29

September 21
Henri Nouwen:
Psalms 16, 23, 42, 62,
71, 91, 100, 116, 121

September 21
International Day of
Prayer and Witness for
Peace:
Psalms 67, 85, 122, 131

September 23
Zechariah, the Father of
St. John the Baptist

September 23
Celebrate Bisexuality Day
Psalms 5, 33, 90, 113,
126, 146

September 26
SS. Cosmas and Damian:
Psalm 126

September 27
St. Vincent de Paul:
Psalm 112

September 28
St. Lawrence Ruiz:
Psalm 34

September 28
Pope John Paul I:
Psalm 103

September 28
St. Wenceslaus:
Psalm 126

September 29
SS. Michael, Gabriel, and
Raphael:
Psalm 138

September 30
St. Jerome:
Psalm 119

Fourth Friday in
September
Peoples Native to the
Americas Day:
Psalms 3, 57, 130

OCTOBER

First Sunday in October
World Communion
Sunday:
Psalms 29, 34, 75,
78, 117

October 1
St. Therese of the
Child Jesus:
Psalm 131

October 2
The Holy Guardian Angels:
Psalm 91

October 4
St. Francis of Assisi:
Psalm 16

October 6
St. Bruno:
Psalm 1

October 6
Blessed Marie Rose
Durocher:
Psalms 1, 34, 128

October 7
Our Lady of the Rosary:
Psalm 42, 131

October 9
St. Denis:
Psalm 126

October 9
St. John Leonardi:
Psalm 96

October 9
Penny Lernoux:
Psalms 11, 15

October 10
National Day for the
Homeless:
Psalm 84

October 19
The Prophet Joel:
Psalm 113

October 19
World Homeless Day
Psalm 84

October 11
St. John XXIII
Psalm 104

October 12
The Syrophoenician
Woman
Psalm 42

October 14
St. Callistus I:
Psalm 40

October 15
St. Teresa of Jesus:
Psalm 19

October 16
St. Hedwig:
Psalm 128

October 16
St. Margaret Mary
Alacoque:
Psalm 23

October 16
World Food Day:
Psalms 65, 145

October 17
St. Ignatius of Antioch:
Psalm 34

October 18
St. Luke:
Psalm 145

October 19
Sts. John De Brébeuf
and Isaac Jogues, and
Companions:
Psalm 126

October 19
Blessed Pope Paul VI
Psalm 104

October 20
St. Paul of the Cross:
Psalm 117

Third Week of October
The National Observance
of Children's Sabbaths:
Psalms 78, 127, 128, 131,

October 21
Hosea:
Psalm 131

October 22
St. John Paul II
Psalm 18

October 23:
St. John of Capistrano:
Psalm 16

October 24
St. Anthony Mary Claret:
Psalm 96

October 24
Rosa Parks:
Psalms 27, 72, 113

October 25
Ruth and Naomi:
Psalm 15, 72, 113

October 26
Noah:
Psalms 8, 136

October 28:
SS. Simon and Jude:
Psalm 19

NOVEMBER

November 1
All Saints / The
Beatitudes
Psalm 15, 24, 103

November 2
Commemoration of All
the Faithful Departed/All
Souls' Day:
Psalms 23, 25, 27

November 3
St. Martin de Porres:
Psalm 131

November 4
St. Charles Borromeo:
Psalm 89

November 5
St. Elizabeth, Mother of
St. John the Baptist-
Psalm 8

November 9
The Dedication of the
Lateran Basilica:
Psalm 46

November 10
St. Leo the Great:
Psalm 37

November 11
St. Martin of Tours:
Psalm 89

November 12
St. Josaphat:
Psalm 1

November 13
St. Frances Xavier
Cabrini:
Psalm 34

November 13
Joseph Cardinal
Bernardin
Psalm 29, 33, 34

November 15
St. Albert the Great:
Psalm 119

November 16
St. Margaret of Scotland:
Psalm 112

November 16
St. Gertrude:
Psalm 23

November 17
St. Elizabeth of Hungary:
Psalm 34

November 18
Dedication of the Basilica
of SS. Peter and Paul:
Psalm 98

November 18
St. Rose Philippine
Duchesne:
Psalm 128

November 21
The Presentation of the
Blessed Virgin Mary:
Psalm 116

November 22
St. Cecilia:
Psalm 45, 126, 149

November 23
St. Clement I:
Psalm 89

November 23
St. Columban:
Psalm 96

November 23
Blessed Miguel Agustin Pro:
Psalm 34

November 24
St. Andrew Dung-Lac:
Psalm 128

November 25
Micah:
Psalms 15, 128

November 27
Harvey Milk:
Psalms 15, 72, 90, 113,
126, 146

November 29
Servant of God
Dorothy Day:
Psalms 11, 34, 116

November 30
St. Andrew:
Psalm 19

November 30
Cities Against the
Death Penalty:
Psalm 27

Fourth Thursday in
November/
Thanksgiving:
Psalm 145

DECEMBER

December 1
World AIDS Day:
Psalms 5, 6, 33, 90, 103,
113, 126, 131, 146

December 2
The Women Martyrs of
El Salvador: Sr. Maura
Clarke, MM; Jean Donovan,
Sr. Ita Ford, MM; Sr.
Dorothy Kazel, OSU:
Psalms 6, 11, 15, 91, 113

December 3
St. Francis Xavier:
Psalm 117

December 4
St. John Damascene:
Psalm 19

December 5
Nelson Mandela:
Psalm 11, 15, 72, 91, 113

December 6
St. Nicholas:
Psalm 40

December 7
St Ambrose:
Psalm 89

December 8
The Immaculate Con-
ception of the Blessed
Virgin Mary:
Psalm 98

December 9
St. Juan Diego
Psalm 124

December 10
Thomas Merton:
Psalm 42, 131, 134

December 10
Universal Declaration of
Human Rights:
Psalms 10, 33, 102

December 11
St. Damasus I:
Psalm 110

December 12
Our Lady of Guadalupe:
Psalm 34

December 13
St. Lucy:
Psalm 31

December 14
St. John of the Cross:
Psalm 37

December 14
Anniversary of the Sandy
Hook Shooting:
Psalms 91, 146

December 15
Judith:
Psalms 147, 148, 149

December 16
Hannah:
Psalm 15, 72, 113

December 17
O Wisdom:
Psalm 80

December 17
Rumi
Psalm 33

December 18
O Sacred Lord of
Ancient Israel:
Psalms 80, 146

December 19
O Flower of Jesse's Stem
Psalms 8, 65, 126

December 20
O Key of David:
Psalm 72

December 21
O Radiant Dawn:
Psalm 5, 25

December 21
St. Peter Canisius:
Psalm 40

December 22
O Sovereign of All the
Nations:
Psalm 117, 126

December 23
O Emmanuel:
Psalms 24, 89

December 23
St. John of Kanty:
Psalm 112

December 24
Christmas Eve /
The Shepherds
Psalms 89, 96

December 25
Christmas / In the
Beginning was the Word
Psalms 96, 98

December 26
St. Stephen:
Psalm 31

December 27
St. John the Evangelist:
Psalm 97

December 28
The Holy Innocents:
Psalm 124

December 29:
St. Thomas Becket:
Psalm 34

December 29
King David, the Psalmist:
Psalms 27, 89, 116, 148,
149, 150

December 30
The Anointing at
Bethany:
Psalms 23, 89

December 31
St. Sylvester:
Psalm 23

MOVABLE FEASTS AND CELEBRATIONS

Passover:
Psalm 136

Rosh Hashanah:
Psalm 149

Yom Kippur:
Psalms 51, 103

Sukkoth:
Psalms 113, 114

Chanukkah:
Psalm 112

Night of Power—
27th Night of Ramadan:
Psalms 96, 100, 115

Gratitude

I am grateful:

To my friend Jim Knipper at Clear Faith Publishing for his lavish generosity and precious friendship.

To Art Zannoni, Fr. Jan Michael Joncas, Fr. Bill Taylor, and Sr. Kathleen Harmon, SNDdeN, for all that I come to learn from them and hold close to my heart about the psalms.

To Betsey Beckman for her free and liberating spirit, which breathes life and movement into everything she prays and proclaims; and to Rory Cooney, for digging deep and offering so many unique windows into expressing what I attempted to do with this project.

To my other spiritual guides, dear friends, and partners in ministry: Bonnie Faber; Sr. Kathleen Storms, SSND; Lori True; Marty Haugen; Fr. Joe Kempf; Sr. Gertrude Foley, SC; Fr. James Bessert; Fr. Ray East; Andrea Goodrich; Lou Anne Tighe; Fr. Raymond Kemp; Jo Infante; Sr. Jo Gaugier, OP; Leisa Anslinger; Fr. George DeCosta; Bill Huebsch; Alissa Hetzner; Matt Reichert; Stephen Petrunak; Kristen Wenzel; Jes Garceau; Matt Maus; Joe Camacho; Bro. Dennis Schmitz; SM. Rob and Mary Glover; Bishop Remi De Roo; Pearl Gervais; Fr. Richard Rohr, OFM; Megan McKenna; Stephen Pishner; Fr. John Forliti; Sr. Edith Prendergast, RC; Robert A. Jonas, Sr. Sue Mosteller, CSJ; Tom Franzak; and Sr. Helen Prejean, CSJ.

To my composer friends and colleagues: first, to Michael, Lori, Marty, Sr. Kathleen, Tom, Rob, and Stephen again; and to Paul Tate; Fr. Ricky Manalo, CSP; Dan Schutte; Gary Daigle; Tony Alonso; Kate Cuddy; Fr. Fran O'Brien; John Foley, SJ; Christopher Walker; Sr. Suzanne Toolan, SM; Paul Inwood; John Bell; Jaime Cortez; Tom Kendzia; Fr. Christopher Willcock, SJ; and Zack Stachowski; and to the composer-psalm servants who have gone before us, such as Fr. Joseph Gelineau, SJ; Fr. Lucien Deiss, and David Clark Isele; and to Leon Roberts—for crafting, creating, and composing such powerful settings of the psalms over the years.

To Maureen Edore at Clear Faith; to Doug Cordes for his design work, to Br. Mickey McGrath for his creative spirit, which adorns the cover of this book; to Leslie Duperon for her initial editing work on the manuscript, and to Kathleen Hollenbeck for her editing and for bringing clarity to my ramblings.

To all of my dear and good friends who are too many to mention here; to Helen, Jeffrey, Colleen and Mary; and to all of my family and relatives in Michigan, Florida, and Utah. There is only love.

Soli Deo Gloria!

DH

About the Author

David Haas is from Eagan, Minnesota, where he is the director of The Emmaus Center for Music, Prayer and Ministry, in addition to serving as the animator for the Taizé Prayer Community at Cretin-Derham Hall in St. Paul, Minnesota. Highly regarded as one of the preeminent composers of liturgical music in the English-speaking world, he has produced and published more than 50 collections and recordings with GIA Publications. His music has been translated into many languages and appears in hymnals of various Christian denominations throughout the world. Among his many popular song-prayers are *Blest Are They*, *You Are Mine*, *We Are Called*, *We Have Been Told*, *Song of the Body of Christ*, *The Name of God*, *Now We Remain*, *Who Calls You By Name*, *Prayer for Peace*, *Deep Within*, *The God of Second Chances*, and *Without Seeing You*.

David is the founder and executive director of *Music Ministry Alive!*, an international liturgical music formation institute for high school and college-age youth (www.musicministryalive.com). He has traveled extensively as a workshop presenter, conference speaker, and concert performer in all 50 states, as well as Canada, Australia, The Bahamas, England, Ireland, Germany, Italy, Israel, Greece, Turkey, and Asia. A collector of icons, he is also the author of more than 30 books in the areas of liturgy and music, prayer and spirituality, religious education, and youth ministry. In 2015, David was the recipient of an Honorary Doctorate in Humane Letters from the University of Portland in Oregon.

To order printed and recorded editions of David's many liturgical compositions, contact:

GIA Publications, Inc.
7404 South Mason Avenue
Chicago, IL 60638
1-800-442-1358
www.giamusic.com

For licensing information of David's music, contact:

www.OneLicense.net
1-800-ONE-1501

45191940R00168

Made in the USA
Middletown, DE
27 June 2017